THE GHOSTS OF
Saint Albans Sanatorium

Pat Bussard O'Keefe

Foreword by Marcelle Hanauer
St. Albans History (1892 – 1911) by Shelli Sprouse Meade

Reaper Publishing
Abingdon, VA

The Ghosts of St. Albans Sanatorium

Reaper Publishing

𝓡

Abingdon, VA 24210

ISBN-13: 978-0692588307 (Reaper Publishing)
ISBN-10: 0692588302

Printed in the United States of America.

Contents

13 Chapters

Appendix

Other

A view of St. Albans

St. Albans

Sanatorium as

seen from across

the New River.

Acknowledgements

Marcelle Hanauer and Shelli Sprouse Meade, St. Albans Sanatorium has called to you, to us. Within these pages, through words and images, we tell her story.

To the teams featured throughout the pages of this book, you are undoubtedly among the best paranormal investigators in the country. Thank you for your willingness to share your experiences with the mistress of darkness known as St. Albans Sanatorium.

To those I owe so much:

My husband Ken, daughters Megan and Stephanie, sisters Pam and Tracey, niece Sam, grandniece and nephew Morgan, and Klaven, you are my heart, my life. You too, Drew, Jon, Eric, and John!

To my new family members, Jaime, Cemal, Jesse, Summer, grandbabies, their grandpa Marc, thank you for making me a part of your lives!

Grandma, Mom, and Marty, although you now walk in the otherworld, I think of you almost daily.

Jennifer, Betsy, and Gayle, good friends are rarer than jewels and more valuable than gold. To my new friends Kathy, Robert, and Scarlett, I hope our friendship grows richer in the years ahead.

A dark history

St. Albans played the gracious hostess to the mad, the sick, the angry, and the demented, who were placed in her care.

According to eye-witness reports, the phantoms of some of them are still there.

A view from the first floor

Imagine the frustration some of the patients must have felt in seeing the outside world from this window, replete with its sunshine and joys, while they sat, warehoused and cloaked in the shadow of St. Albans.

foreword

St. Albans Sanatorium has a beautiful Sphinx-like presence that literally vibrates with remarkable energy. She will often call out to certain people, pulling them into her arms and into her service. I know, because she chose me to help save her and I am not alone.

When I first came to St. Albans I was working with merchandising. At that time I was afraid of the dark hallways and empty rooms of the old asylum. I quickly overcame my fear and this emotion was replaced by a love of the building and what it meant for so many who had come before me.

We are its caretakers. Those of us, both paid and volunteer who strive to keep the doors open to a place worth saving, a place that was once the custodian to so many within its care.

Those of us who are now here carry on the vision of people like Don Hanauer, former Director of Operations for St. Albans. He saw the beauty in this building and had a vision of restoring it to its former glory. As outlined in the final chapter of this book, we have worked on a number of special events developed to generate funding for the structure's restoration.

At some point, Don's vision for St. Albans became mine. After Don left, I knew that I would need to lead the effort to take the sanatorium from disrepair back into wholeness. The beauty and spirit of this historic landmark now draws paranormal investigators from all over America and beyond, to walk the hallways with the intent of encountering its remaining residents.

Not one paranormal investigator, staff, or volunteer, spends time within the structure of St. Albans without meeting some of those Spirits, myself included. I have several stories to share, but I will impart only two within the pages of this book.

Decaying Beauty

The St. Albans Sanatorium team, volunteers, and owner have worked hard to renovate and save this architectural gem.

I was working late one night when I noticed one of our volunteers, Shelli Sprouse Meade, on the camera monitoring system coming into the building. But, when we looked for her, we couldn't find her anywhere in the building. The next day when I saw her, I asked why she had checked in the night before. Her response was chilling. She said that she hadn't been to St. Albans the night before. She had been so exhausted that she had fallen asleep fully clothed and was still asleep at the time we saw her in the building. She also described what she had on when she had fallen asleep. They were the very clothes I had seen her wearing while walking past the monitor the night before.

On another occasion, when I was at the sanatorium by myself with my office door closed, I began to hear footsteps pacing back and forth. I looked up from my monitor and noticed a shadow keeping time with the footsteps, on the other side of the closed portal. Eventually, the footsteps dissipated. I was a bit unnerved. But, this is after all, the very haunted St. Albans Sanatorium.

When I first met Pat Bussard O'Keefe, I was struck by her professionalism. She had written a brilliant article about St. Albans titled, *A Repository of Souls* for Ghost Voices Magazine and I was impressed by her passionate words and lovely images of the sanatorium. When I saw her photography illustrating the article, I knew that she was able to capture images of St. Albans as she really is, almost alive with energy. When she told me that she would like to write a book about the old sanatorium, I was immediately excited about the prospect of a publication that would feature images providing a window into the soul of the asylum. Those images, combined with the stories of paranormal investigators who have come seeking a connection to the Spirits who reside here and have found it, provides a historical and haunted perspective of this beloved place. The Ghosts of St. Albans Sanatorium will give readers an insight into the attraction of the building for those seeking an encounter with spirit energy.

There are so many people to thank for trying to salvage St. Albans before she slipped into total disrepair and faded away into oblivion, like some other important but unfortunate buildings of historic and paranormal repute. Among those special people are Don Hanauer, Chuck Thornton, my brother David, Barry O'Dell and Mountain Ridge Paranormal Research Society, and a number of amazingly dedicated volunteers too numerous to list here. To each of you, I thank you for the love you have shown to the Spirit of St. Albans.

Future home of the St. Albans Museum

Visitors who came

prior to 2015

wouldn't recognize

the area to the right

of the King Center

entrance. Much

work was done to

make this area the

future home of the

SAS Museum.

I would like to give a special thanks to Shelli Sprouse Meade who wrote the history of St. Albans in its formative years as a boys school, from 1892 – 1911. This part of the sanatorium's history is featured as part of the first chapter of the book. *A Repository of Souls: A History of St. Albans Sanatorium*, which gives the reader an understanding of the evolution of the site, from boys' school to paranormal destination, and a snapshot of the people who were linked to her over the decades of the building's existence.

Sitting on the banks of the New River, the sanatorium has stood guard over Radford, Virginia since opening its doors in 1892. The Ghosts of St. Albans Sanatorium will help to ensure that her haunted heritage is immortalized.

Haunted buildings never die as long as their stories are preserved and remembered.

Marcelle Hanauer
Director of Operations
St. Albans Sanatorium
www.stalbans-virginia.com

St. Albans Sanatorium

WWW.STALBANS-VIRGINIA.COM

Director of Operations

Marcelle Hanauer stands in front of a poster of St. Albans Sanatorium.

Introduction

Come with me as I take you inside one of the most unsung haunted locations in the United States today. It is a journey down dark hallways and into rooms painted by both shadow and light where spirits talk and phantoms walk.

St. Albans Sanatorium is a destination known by serious paranormal investigators as a place where they can seek answers to the mysteries of what lies beyond death. Some of these investigators were able to find resolutions for themselves to a number of these age old riddles through their experiences at the sanatorium. The frightening and true stories found within the pages of this book are about these inquisitive investigators' encounters with The Ghosts of St. Albans Sanatorium.

In addition, Shelli Sprouse Meade explores the sanatorium's first two decades, which are compiled along with historical information provided by St. Albans staff, to create a brief history of the now defunct asylum in the first chapter of the book. St Albans had several incarnations over the decades between the years of 1892, when she opened, and her final day of operation near the turn of a new century. Some of those lifetimes included serving as a boys' school, a warehouse for those with addictions and mental illnesses, a location used by Radford University for art classes, doctor's offices, and finally, as a paranormal destination for all who dare enter into her waiting embrace. In all of her lifetimes she has cradled each selected soul who has come through her foyer as if to keep them dear to her, forever.

When I initially encountered the energy that is St. Albans Sanatorium, I was on assignment for Ghost Voices Magazine, a now defunct publication with headquarters in the United Kingdom. As I slowly drove up the driveway that first takes you in back and then in front of the building, I noticed a calm about the structure, reminiscent of the long, lazy days of a southern summer.

Exterior of St. Albans Sanatorium, riverfront, far right

This stunning

example of Victorian

architecture sits on

the banks of the

mighty New River.

The kind of summer known for the wafting scent of sweet magnolias, languid bouts of love making, and heat so burning you can see it in energetic waves lifting from asphalt roads. St. Albans Sanatorium was calm on the surface, but just inside her doors vibrated the kind of energy necessary to mask dark secrets and horrors untold, safely hidden within cold rooms, long unused.

I was instantly smitten by her energy and knew that one day I would write part of her story, beyond the magazine assignment I was originally sent there to compose. St. Albans Sanatorium called to me as she is wont to do when she wishes a task completed. I heard her call and answered.

Over the years since my original visit, I have made many trips to the old sanatorium. I never tire of her aging beauty, or the energy that permeates every square inch of her structure. She is like a good book that one reads then reads again, only to discover magical elements that went unnoticed during the first examination. Each time I visit, I am more in awe of her beauty and her power.

Like most people who spend a lengthy amount of time within her walls, I have tales to tell. I will share with you a personal experience I had on March 25, 2012 when I and another investigator, Jennifer Woodward Proffitt of HAUNT Paranormal, were taking an investigative tour of the building. Our guide that night was a member of Mountain Ridge Paranormal Research Society (MRPRS).

We were on the second floor and had entered into an area where the notable traits were peeling paint and two short hallways, behind which were small rooms capped by metal doors. We were told by our guide that this is where the completely mentally unstable were housed during the time that St. Albans served as a sanatorium. It was where the worst of the worst patients were kept.

I suddenly felt something to my left. Because I am a photographer, as well as a writer, I tend to keep my camera to my eye most of the time when on an investigation, or covering a story.

I swung towards where I had felt the movement take place in the darkness and saw something in the camera's viewfinder that I will never forget and still haunts me to this day. I saw, very plainly, an old woman's face that was twisted in the most horrific mask of hate and rage that one can imagine and this face was focusing those emotions on me. This push of energy was palatable. In that moment, at 2:01 a.m., on March 25, 2012, I pushed the shutter release on my camera and caught a photo of something indistinct. Unfortunately, the photo does have a longer exposure, so it is not

Paranormal laboratory

The former asylum is the perfect location to conduct experiments focused on finding answers to the supernatural.

indisputable evidence of a paranormal encounter. I have shared this photo below for your consideration.

There are several other stories that I wish to share with you, but I will do so in Chapter 12, *It's All in the Photographs: The Ghost Writers*. My daughters Stephanie and Megan, Ken O'Keefe, Scarlett McGrady, Jon Matney, and I make up the key members of this team of paranormal investigators. Cheyenne McGrady, Pamela Wilson Berry and Leigh Schilling Edwards, serve as auxiliary members.

During a photo shoot on November 1, 2014, at St. Albans I took a series of photographs of what appeared to be a white mist (ectoplasm) as it developed into a humanoid form. I also share those photos with you in that chapter.

Our encounters with the ghastly and glorious ghosts of St. Albans are fairly typical of the experiences of the other paranormal investigative teams you will read about in The Ghosts of St. Albans Sanatorium.

So, sit down with me and read a spell. Follow my words as we go deep into the recesses of this dark lady of the paranormal, the lovely and haunted St. Albans Sanatorium. As you read, I hope that you can vicariously experience the encounter between investigator and Spirit.

Pat Bussard O'Keefe

The Haunted Photographer

www.patbussard.com

**Author,
Photographer,
Psychic Medium**

Pat Bussard O'Keefe

at the riverside

entrance to St.

Albans Sanatorium.

*All photographs by

O'Keefe, unless

otherwise noted.

Most of the team

photos were provided

courtesy of the

investigators.

Sentinels

Columns on the
exterior of the
sanatorium,
riverfront.

Meet (some of) the Ghosts and Entities

Jacob – A young boy of about eight who is thought to have been murdered by a pedophiliac orderly named Donald in the 1970s. Jacob is an active little spirit in the asylum. He is known to try to push people out of his way who get too close. For those who would like to meet him, ascend the grand staircase, and take a right at the second floor landing. Donald's room is immediately in front of the viewer. Enter this room and stand approximately 18 inches from the right hand wall (the wall to the right upon entering the room). Be patient and see if Jacob responds. He is often heard on EVPs and his presence can also be felt in his room and around the building by those who are sensitive to spirit energy.

Rebecca – A young woman in her late twenties or thirties, who hung herself in the "suicide bathroom" on the third floor of the sanatorium. She often tries to connect with investigators. Although often seen and heard on the floor where she perished, she is also reported as a lady in white ascending the grand staircase.

Alley, of the Bowling Alley – This sweet spirit was reported playing in the bowling alley by a number of witnesses. Reports of her laughing and giggling are rather common. According to SAS staff, a police officer had his flashlight lifted out of his pocket in the bowling alley. It scared him so badly, that he refused to come back. It is unknown if Alley was responsible for that contact.

The Tall Man – This being is a tall shadow figure that is especially active on the grand staircase, although he is seen throughout the building.

Tongue Man – A usually friendly ghost whose nickname was given because his tongue protrudes awkwardly from his mouth, in the fashion of those on heavy psychiatric medication. He is reported wandering throughout the second floor and beyond.

The Growler – A being that growls aggressively at visitors to St. Albans. It is encountered in the bowling alley and more infrequently, in other parts of the building.

Hat Man – This shadow being is reported on the second floor near the elevators. It is a very powerful entity, whose bearing is almost regal. Most who encounter this shadow being report a feeling of dread.

The Creeper – These are shadow beings that can climb walls and are often spotted on all fours scurrying in and out of rooms before disappearing into shadows and walls.

The Smiler – An investigator reported seeing this being fall from the ceiling, suspending itself while upside down right in front of the man's face. As if that wasn't shocking enough, the creature flashed an evil grin at him before disappearing once again into the shadows.

Confederate and Union Soldiers – A paranormal investigator reported a Confederate soldier who appeared to be wandering aimlessly on the first floor of the building. Union soldiers have also been seen, camped outside where the parking lot is located riverside.

Anonymous Children – The laughter and footsteps of unidentified children have been heard by investigators in the building.

Ghostly Staff and Patients – A nurse has been reported walking straight through the skylight hallway towards the grand staircase, then turning and walking into what is now known as the rainbow room. Ghostly staff and patients have been reported on all of the floors at St. Albans.

Older Gentleman – This ghostly specter was found crouched in the corner of the file room, as if hiding from someone, or something.

Disembodied Sounds – The shuffling of papers are often heard in the file room. The sounds were so loud on one night that the police were called. The officer who arrived at St. Albans that evening also heard the sounds of, what may be, someone forever at work. Talking, laughing, and direct verbal communication by spirits with individuals have been reported.

Disappearing Doorway – Investigators were in the "safe room," (a room that housed an old safe) when they got up to leave, the door had disappeared. Details are provided in Chapter 11.

Disappearing Hallway– This paranormal anomaly was witnessed by the author and two other investigators, on September 27, 2015, at approximately 4:00 p.m. Details are provided in Chapter 12.

Chapter 1
Repository of Souls

History of St Albans Sanatorium

Years 1892 - 1911
By: Shelli Sprouse Meade

Years 1912 to Present
Courtesy of St Albans Sanatorium

St. Albans Sanatorium exudes history through every rock, brick, timber, partition, façade, and layer of paint. It is a history of chronological facts and events, certainly, but it is also a history of people and their experiences, and the traces of themselves that have been left behind. Visitors ask questions, and volunteers do their best to answer them. What treatments were performed? How many people died here? Is it haunted? Did *you* ever have a paranormal experience here? All too often the answer is simply that we cannot truly know.

Perhaps it is simply human nature to try to find answers, to fill in the blanks. So we research, and we interview what eyewitnesses we can find. We theorize, and yes, even speculate. What evolves is a patchwork of a shroud, stitched together from facts, anecdotes, impressions, logical interpretation, personal experiences, and opinions. All of these are layered over the building protectively by the volunteers and other supporters who have dedicated themselves to preserving and extending the vitality of St. Albans Sanatorium.

St. Albans School, 1892-1911

St. Albans began as a private preparatory high school for boys under the ownership and leadership of Professor George W. Miles. Two buildings were designed by Philadelphia architect Mantle Fielding and constructed in the Colonial style between 1890 and 1892, the larger of which became known as "The Home" (aka, Catherine Hall) and the smaller, "The Hall." The first term of St. Albans School commenced September 19, 1892.

Professor George Miles
The Promus, 1895-96

The city of Radford was incorporated that same year when West Radford and the town of Radford merged to create a population over 5,000. Radford had been experiencing great population and industry growth, facilitated by the railroad and the Central Depot, a halfway point between

The home and the hall

The primary residence is pictured in the background with the hall in the foreground, which served as a study and reading space on the first floor and dormitories on the second floor.

Scanned Photos are courtesy of Glencoe Museum.

The two color photos to the right are recent images of St. Albans Sanatorium.

Lynchburg and Bristol. Incoming students to St. Albans School would have likely found Radford to be a growing area, perhaps a bit full of its own potential importance, much like the general spirit of the boys, themselves.

Professor Miles recruited young men of athletic ability, and St. Albans School developed a formidable reputation for its many sporting teams. The school yearbook, The Promus, was written by the students each year and consistently featured clubs and athletic teams, with detailed descriptions of wins and losses. Consistent with St. Albans' reputation as a premier preparatory school of the South, intellectual and artistic pursuits are evident as well. The boys also seemed to enjoy integrating with the city of Radford and engaging socially with local young people, including young ladies, who were invited to functions at the school and even contributed occasionally to the yearbook. The Promus is filled with the often mischievous spirits of the young men who once lived, laughed, schemed, and dreamed at St. Albans.

• • •

The Albans Ghosts

To J.C.B.

The Master sat in his easy chair,
The study-hall lamps burnt bright.
But little he knew that a horrid crew
Were marshaling just out of sight.

Harry opened the door when across the floor,
With a stride both bold and grim.
Come Peters, the great, straight onto the fate
The Master had waiting for him.

When Charley walked in, a mighty din
Shook the windows again and again
While Harry and Frank enjoyed the prank
And followed with smirks and a grin.

These four came on, with chatter and groan,
To "queer" the Master and boys.
In burnt cork and sheets they walked the streets
And made a ghost-like noise.

The scheme went awry, they were *caught on the fly*,
In the study-hall they sat quite awhile;
Thirty days on the lot, helped to spoil the plot;
Of demerits, they rolled up a pile.

Next day at their posts, these merry ghosts
Felt akin to Hamlet's sire;
For, purging away the crimes of that day
They thought they "fasted in fire."

The Albans Ghosts
An original poem from the 1893-1894
issue of The Promus.

• • •

Victorian details

The sumptuous wood and gorgeous details found in unexpected places mark this building's origination in the Victorian era. Pictured is a visual slice of an ornate steam heat radiator.

"I Will"

Have you seen the white rose petal
When dew-drops deck its stem?
Or plucked a young apple blossom
As it nestles, a tiny gem?

Have you breathed in the depths of the
wild-wood
The wind from arbutus beds?
Or walked mid the meadow grasses
Where violets lift their heads?

Have you played in the surge of the ocean
And caught the foamy crests?
Or smoothed the young dove's feathers
Asleep in their wind-rocked nests?

Have you watched the milky whiteness
Of a cloud that the sun distils,
And caught the tinted glories
Of a rainbow on the hills?

Such beauties but hint of the glories
When her cheeks with blushes fill
And her sweet breath faintly murmurs
Close down on my breast, "I will."

"I Will"

An original poem from the 1893 – 1894

Issue of <u>The Promus</u>.

St. Albans School was a very orderly institution, similar to a military school. The students regularly attended a morning gymnasium drill under the direction of one of the four Masters (Professors). The total number of boarding students was limited to 50. One characteristic that made St. Albans unique was a focus on the students being part of the family of the headmaster. Young men were expected to conduct themselves appropriately, sharing meals with the headmaster's family. Professor Miles left St. Albans School in either 1902 or 1903, maintaining ownership but leasing the buildings to Winslow H. Randolph, a reputable educator, who would also serve as Headmaster. Miles' reasons for leaving are unclear, attributed to possibly business or employment opportunities elsewhere and/or his health. Randolph served as Headmaster for at least one full term (1903–1904).

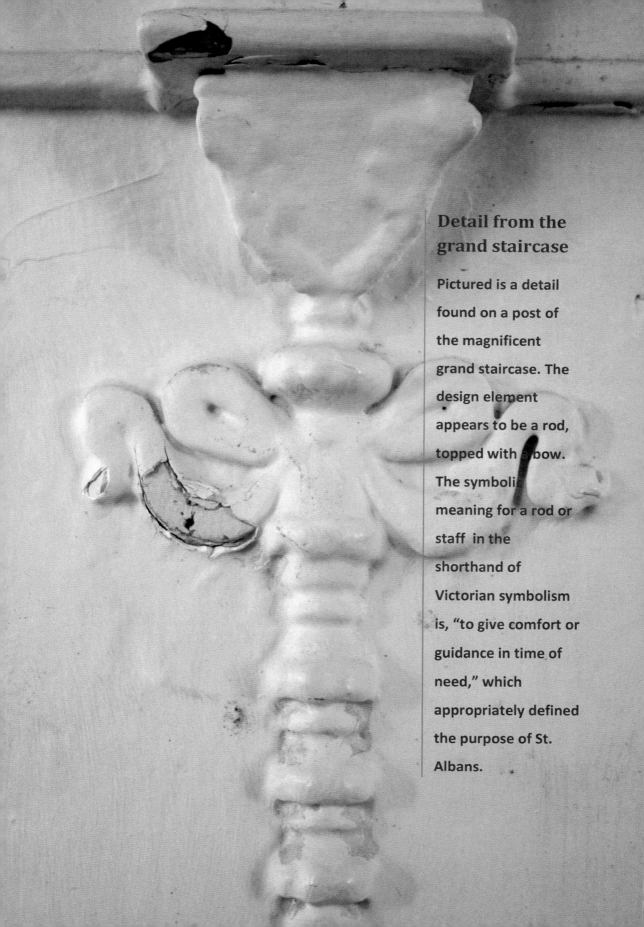

Detail from the grand staircase

Pictured is a detail found on a post of the magnificent grand staircase. The design element appears to be a rod, topped with a bow. The symbolic meaning for a rod or staff in the shorthand of Victorian symbolism is, "to give comfort or guidance in time of need," which appropriately defined the purpose of St. Albans.

THE TIMES—DISPATCH: RICHMOND, VA., SATURDAY, SEPTEMBER 17, 1904.

Plans were clearly in place to continue the school for the 1904-1905 term, as evidenced by no less than 24 advertisements posted in *The Richmond Times Dispatch* during June, July, August, and September 1904. The ads list Randolph as Headmaster. Despite these intentions, it was announced that St. Albans would close in September 1904, just after the new term was scheduled to start, due to a "change in management" and lack of students. It seems that Professor Miles was so integral to the very nature and spirit of St. Albans School that it could not survive without him.

While the closing announcement also clearly states that it was Professor Miles' intention to return to St. Albans School and revive it, that intention was never realized. It was reported in February 1905 that Professor Miles was hospitalized in Richmond and very ill. Despite x-ray treatment (the precursor to radiation

ST. ALBANS TO CLOSE.

Colonel Miles Will Later Again Take Charge and Revive It.

(Special to The Times-Dispatch.)

RADFORD, VA., Sept. 16.—Because of a change of management and the general patronage, it has been decided to close St. Albans school for the present session.

The shutting down of any industrial plant would not be attended by the profound regret with which this announcement has been received. This is the academy that was built by Colonel George W. Miles twelve years ago, and from its very first session took its place as one of the first training schools of the Southern States. For ten years, while under the immediate direction and management of Colonel Miles it had an uninterrupted succession of successful sessions. In fact, Colonel Miles had so interwoven his life into the life of the school that his withdrawal from the active management of the same caused an immediate falling off of its patronage. In fact, he was the school. The beautiful colonial buildings, the commanding site, the healthful and high altitude makes an ideal spot for a school, and it is gratifying in the midst of our disappointment at its closing, to learn that large plans are being formed for its continued usefulness hereafter. Colonel Miles has consented to take personal supervision of the selection of its teachers and the enlistment of its patronage hereafter, and will furnish the means for its proper advertisement and restoration.

As the school was a child of his brain, the people of Radford naturally look to him to restore it to its strength and full share of usefulness.

The school is incorporated for $25,000 capital stock and also has $15,000 of first mortgage bonds all owned by the founder, Colonel George W. Miles, as well as a greater part of the stock.

Two years ago Colonel Miles turned over the entire management of the school, including its financial management, discipline, patronage, and course of study, together with an option on the stock, but has now assumed control again, and will become personally identified with its destinies.

therapy), Professor George W. Miles died February 26, 1905 of liver cancer.

The tone of reporting of the time suggests that the general community was genuinely regretful about the loss of St. Albans School and Professor Miles. Certainly the school had increased local commerce and revenue, but it was also a source of pride to the general community, having received many accolades for its preparation of young men for post-secondary education or business. This was the first time that the buildings stood empty and the future of the site uncertain.

St. Albans History 1892 – 1911, by Shelli Sprouse Meade

Richmond Manufactures

obacco, Baking Powder, Meat Juices, ıks, Bags, Saddlery, Harness, Hats, s, Paper, Paper Boxes. Wooden Ware, s and Spokes, Tin Tags and Boxes, Tin ing, Fertilizers, Agricultural Implements, seshoes, Nails, Railroad Spikes, Car s, Locomotives, Stoves, Etc. Twenty-million dollars invested in manufactur-annual output, $60,000,000.

Southern Merchants

Can Buy Their

Fall and Winter Stocks

To Best Advantage

When They Visit

Richmond Wholesal

Dry Goods, Notions, Milliner Shoes, Hats, Caps, Clothing, Provisions, Liquors, Tobacco, Dru ware, Railway, Mill and Plumbers' Seeds, Stoves, Tin, Hides, Leather, and Saddlery, Books, Stationery, Ware, Carpets, Straw Goods, Etc. a half million dollras invested; bus year, $43,400,789.

The South's Greatest Wholesale Market

RICHMOND

The Trade Center of the Southern States

Special Advantages

chmond has seven great railroad lines and boat lines with direct connections with steamship lines. giving lowest competi-reight rates and quickest service over all Every line merchandise is represented e city's manufacturers and wholesalers. al inducements in the way of terms and to Southern buyers.

They Can Save Money

On Prices and on Freight;

Can Get Goods Quickly

Either by Rail or Water.

You're Invited!

Railroad Fare Paid

Leading manufacturers and merch refund the railroad fare of any South chant buying goods of them. Merch ing advantage of this offer should r Chamber of Commerce promptly u val in the city. Full information this offer may be had by addres Chamber of Commerce, Richmond,

MASSENGALE ADVERTISING AGENCY.

ROAD TO ...CKSBURG

... Anthracite Com... Runs Its First Train.

... TO GUESTS

...Day for Christians...burg and the Vir...technic Institute.

...he Times-Dispatch.)
...URG, VA., September 16. ...nthracite Coal and Rail... ran its first passenger ...sburg yesterday and for... line for the transaction

... some time in the fifties ...btained for a road from ...epot to Blacksbur, and ... this various plans have ... under numerous cha... ...struction of a railroad, ...mounted to nothing. In ..., the attention of Mr. W. ...ur city, was directed to ...n the Price and Brush ...s county, a new charter ... a railroad, and it soon ... that the enterprise had ...e the hands of one who ... a successful conclusion. ... delays incident to pro... ...way, on the 11th day of ... the work of construc... ...and the road completed ...distance of five and one... ...pril, 1903.

...COAL MINES.

...ad been operated in a ... number of years, but ...anagement the most ap...-date methods were in...rge breaker, with a ca... per day, has been erect... successful operation.

... constructed after the ...nd produces seven sizes ... the Pennsylvania stand...chinery, appliances and ... the mines were select... place under the super... R. Wilson, the general ...cated and experienced ... from the Pennsylvania

... present is rather small ...ty in procuring suitable ...mpany is now working ... will increase the num... ... possible to four times ...o enable it to meet the ...coal which cannot now

...Blacksburg were so car... in their entreaties that ... be completed to their ...management finally de...o, and on the 11th day ...ork was commenced on ... the rails laid into the ...his month.

Phlegar, W. C. Flagg, J. R. Eoff, W. L. Currin, J. R. Johnson, J. H. Thompson, W. M. Dunklee, W. F. Tallant, R. B. Spindle and Dr. A. S. Ellett, prominent citizens of Christiansburg; Mr. W. H. Tomney, of the Roanoke Times, and Mrs. J. R. Wilson and Miss Laura Jordan, boarded the first passenger coach to run over the road. At the station they were joined by W. J. Payne, vice-president; L. G. Crenshaw, auditor; Guy F. Ellett, secretary, and J. W. Walters and G. W. Walters, of the directorate.

The train, in charge of Engineman A. P. Witt, Fireman Grayson Lucas and Conductor C. R. Fagg, commenced its first journey and reached Blacksburg after a delightful run of about 40 minutes. On approaching the latter place, Engineman Witt awakened the echoes, as well as the natives, by a prolonged whistle from his locomotive, and amid the wavin gof handkerchiefs and other manifestations of delight from a large crowd which had assembled, the train pulled up to the temporary station. After a stay of half an hour, the return trip was commenced, the party being joined by Dr. and Mrs. J. M. McBryde, Professor and Mrs. L. S. Randolph, Professor and Mrs. W. D. Saunders, Professor and Mrs. Vawter, Professor and Mrs. R. J. Davidson, all of the Virginia Polytechnic Institute; Mr. and Mrs. Wirt Dunlap and many other ladies and gentlemen.

A GREAT BOON.

Only those who are compelled to travel the nine miles of almost impassible mountain road, during the cold, bleak, dreary winter months, can fully appreciate what the opening of this new road means.

Convenient schedules will be arranged so that passengers by the Norfolk and Western train can make close connection to and from Blacksburg.

The Virginia Anthracite Coal Company owns very valuable coal lands on the Brush Mountain, and it is only a question of time when the road will be extended so as to open up those fields and bring into the market a quality of coal that cannot be surpassed for domestic purposes. J.

Wysor Scares Slemp.

(Special to The Times-Dispatch.)

BRISTOL, VA., Sept. 16.—Seeing that the Democrats are determined to elect Joseph C. Wysor to Congress from the Ninth Virginia district, if possible, Congressman Slemp, the Republican nominee, has become quite active, and is making speeches every day. He has been in Washington county, near Bristol, this week. Hon. P. H. McCaull, who was the Republican nominee for Governor of Virginia in 1897, has come to the district to aid Colonel Slemp, and is making speeches. The contest grows warmer as the days go by, and it is destined to be the hottest fight ever waged in the district. While Wysor's chances have improved apparently, it is by no means certain that he will sweep the district, as is predicted by some of his enthusiastic admirers.

Green Bay Leaves.

(Special to The Times-Dispatch.)

GREEN BAY, VA., Sept. 16.—Rev. F. W. Berry continues very sick with congestion of the brain and stomach. But little hope is entertained.

Valuable ores have been found on the lands of Mr. Louis Liertner, two miles north of this place, and if same can be found in large quantities work will be commenced and the ore marketed, as the property is only three hundred yards from railroad siding and can be marketed at a very small expense.

A large number of German families are buying land and settling in this community, and, as a whole, they make a very desirable class of citizens.

GO ON THE POPULAR TRILBY THE BEST ROUTE

TO NORFOLK, OCEAN VIEW AND VA. BEACH TO-MORROW.

$1.00 round trip to Norfolk and Ocean View. $1.25 to Virginia Beach. Quickest

PETERSBURG IS HONORED

Brief Sketch of the Two Officers Chosen by the Grand Camp.

MANY SUPPLY LIENS

American Tobacco Co. Concentrating Its Manufacturing Business in Cockade City.

(Special to The Times-Dispatch.)

PETERSBURG, VA., Sept. 16.—Petersburg has been highly honored by the Grand Camp of Confederate Veterans in electing two of her most distinguished citizens as officers and selecting this city as the next place of meeting.

Dr. W. E. Harwood, of this city, who was to-day elected Grand Commander, is one of the most prominent physicians here and a highly esteemed citizen. When Petersburg was attacked by Federal cavalry under Colonel Kautz, in June, 1864, Dr. Harwood was a schoolboy here, and bore a gallant part in the heroic defense made by that noble band of men and boys who volunteered for the memorable battle of June 9, 1864, when that small army, like the "Dauntless Three," of Rome, withheld the enemy at the city's gates.

The election of Dr. John Herbert Claiborne as Surgeon-General adds another to the many honors awarded to this well known soldier and scientist. Dr. Claiborne is a physician of widespread reputation, whose ability as a practitioner and author of medical treatises has long since placed him in the first rank of his profession.

MANY LIENS.

Supply liens against the Virginia Passenger and Power Company, to the number of nearly a hundred, have been filed here in the office of the clerk of the court. The amounts vary greatly and aggregate nearly $60,000, many of which claims are made by Richmond parties.

The tobacco market here is very quiet, with only a few sales of primings and regular sales at the warehouses will not begin until about the middle of October.

CONCENTRATION.

It seems quite evident to business men, tobacconists and others that the big allied tobacco companies, American and others, are concentrating a large amount of business in Petersburg, a fact that is often attested by their continued operation of hitherto independent manufactories.

The pursuance of such a policy can produce great and important results in Petersburg, making it a manufacturing center of one of the greatest corporations in the world, largely increasing the volume of business, adding greatly to freight shipments from this city over the three big railroads running herein, and creating a sure demand for labor, both white and colored.

The movement to make Petersburg a big bright tobacco market during the coming season is but one of many of like commercial and economic influences try, demanding supplies and labor in a community.

The steamer Brandon, of the Old Dominion Line, which ran aground near City Point during the big storm on Wednesday night, was floated last night undamaged.

The sudden freshet in the Appomattox caused by the storm continues, and the river is still rising and has flooded portions of River Street and caused considerable damage along the wharves.

ST. ALBANS TO CLOSE.

Colonel Miles Will Later Again Take Charge and Revive It.

(Special to The Times-Dispatch.)

RADFORD, VA., Sept. 16.—Because of a change of management and the ... patronage, it has been decided to close St. Albans school for the present session.

The shutting down of any industrial plant would not be attended by the profound regret with which this announcement has been received. This is the academy that was built by Colonel George W. Miles twelve years ago, and from its very first session took its place as one of the first training schools of the Southern States. For ten years, while under the immediate direction and management of Colonel Miles it had an uninterrupted succession of successful sessions, in fact, Colonel Miles had so interwoven his life into the life of the school that his withdrawal from the active management of the same caused an immediate falling off of its patronage. In fact, he was the school. The beautiful colonial buildings, the commanding site, the healthful and high altitude makes an ideal spot for a school, and it is gratifying in the midst of our disappointment at its closing, to learn that large plans are being formed for its continued usefulness hereafter. Colonel Miles has consented to take personal supervision of the selection of its teachers and the enlistment of its patronage hereafter, and will furnish the means for its proper advertisement and restoration.

As the school was a child of his brain, the people of Radford naturally look to him to restore it to its strength and full share of usefulness.

The school is incorporated for $25,000 capital stock and also has $15,000 of first mortgage bonds all owned by the founder, Colonel George W. Miles, as well as a greater part of the stock.

Two years ago Colonel Miles turned over the entire management of the school, including its financial management, discipline, patronage, and course of study, together with an option on the stock, but has now assumed control again, and will become personally identified with its destinies.

COLLEGE OPENED.

Large Party of Californians to Visit Battlefields.

(Special to The Times-Dispatch.)

FREDERICKSBURG, VA., Sept. 16.—Fredericksburg College has opened for the session under the most favorable auspices and with a large attendance. Among the new members of the faculty are Mr. W. O. Ryburn, of Halifax county, in the department of Greek and English; Miss Doggett, music; Miss Epps, primary department. The buildings of the college have all been handsomely repainted and renovated and present a handsome appearance.

The City Council last night made an appropriation of $160 to Fredericksburg College for ten scholarships for pupils from the public schools of this city to be selected by the merit system.

A party of seventy Californians will visit this city on Saturday, September 24th. They have arranged for a drive over the city, visiting historic points, and they will also go over a portion of the battlefields. They will go from here to Richmond.

Dixon—Fitchett.

(Special to The Times-Dispatch.)

CAPE CHARLES, VA., Sept. 16.—Mr. W. W. Dixon and Miss Harriett Fitchett, daughter of Mr. and Mrs. W. C. Fitchett, of Copeville, were married in the Methodist church at that place Wednesday, Rev. W. P. Wright officiating.

Robson—Ellis.

(Special to The Times-Dispatch.)

STAUNTON, VA., Sept. 16.—A very pretty wedding took place Wednesday evening at the Presbyterian church at Mossy Creek, when, at 4 o'clock, Miss Annie Graham Ellis, late of Indian Territory, became the bride of Mr. ...

A BOY OF ELEVEN CLEARED OF MURDER

Killed Another Boy of His Own Age With a Rock.

(Special to The Times-Dispatch.)

CHESTERFIELD, VA., Sept. 16.—Young Elijah Steger was tried in the Circuit Court to-day for killing Robert Young (both colored) on July 11th, and acquitted.

Mr. Charles L. Page represented the little prisoner, who gave his age as not quite eleven, being one of the youngest persons ever prosecuted here for a felony. The story of the killing of Young, as related in court, was to the effect that Steger, when driving his cows home on the day of the trouble, was met by Robert Young and other boys in search of their cattle. Steger's cows were run out of the road into the bushes, causing some unpleasantness. A few "knocks" passed, and when they got a few paces apart a rock or two was exchanged between Steger and Young. The latter was struck back of the ear, stunned and mortally wounded, dying next day of fracture of the skull.

The Commonwealth's testimony indicated a malicious spirit on the prisoner's part towards this particular boy he killed, as shown by a threat he made and other circumstances, but the jury declined to convict one so young of intentional murder. The case consumed the whole day.

The civil docket for this term will be arranged about next Wednesday, if court continues into next week, as now proposed.

Hon. C. W. Waddy, who, with Judge Gregory, was counsel for the plaintiff in the suit of Bessie Lozon against the Atlantic Coast Line Railroad Company, which was tried at the last term and resulted in a hung jury, was at the courthouse to-day arranging for a new trial at this term. The suit was for $15,000 for bodily injuries.

Gus Rableski will be tried to-morrow for felonious assault.

The will of the late B. L. Hargrove was admitted to probate by the county clerk yesterday.

Mrs. Richard Briggs arrived here yesterday from Norfolk and is stopping at Hon. P. V. Cogbill's.

VA. FEMALE INSTITUTE.

United Brethren Congregation to Rebuild Their Church.

(Special to The Times-Dispatch.)

STAUNTON, VA., Sept. 16.—The Virginia Female Institute opened Wednesday for its sixty-first session. Miss Harris and Miss Stuart, teachers, spent the summer in Holland, and Miss Walker in St. Louis.

The buildings have been painted in Colonial colors of buff and white, its original dress. A new four-story brick addition in the rear, contains two recitation rooms, large halls and stairways, and a number of bath rooms. A large and beautiful stone wall has been built at the foot of the east lawn, which presents a beautiful picture.

The trustees of the United Brethren Church, of this city, have closed a contract with the firm of Larner and Smith for rebuilding their edifice on West Street. The contract price is $8,700. When completed this will be a handsome building.

A PAINFUL ACCIDENT.

Prominent Citizen Nearly Loses His Nose in a Canning Factory.

(Special to The Times-Dispatch.)

MONTROSS, VA., Sept. 16.—Mr. A. M. ... in the canning factory here, of which he is part owner. The handle of a flying crank struck him on the nose, almost entirely severing it from his face. Had he been an inch nearer the crank, he would have been instantly killed.

Rev. Dr. John Hannon, of Trinity Methodist Episcopal Church, Richmond, is here assisting the pastor, Rev. J. W. Fizer, in a reival meeting at Andrew Chapel, Methodist Episcopal Church, at this place. Large crowds are in attendance and a great revival is expected. Rev. R. P. Lumpkin, of Epworth Methodist Episcopal Church, Richmond, is expected to assist in the meeting.

Mrs. E. T. Mann, of Richmond, is visiting her son, Dr. G. C. Mann, of this place.

A Splendid Revival.

(Special to The Times-Dispatch.)

MORRISVILLE, VA., Sept. 16.—One of the most notable revivals ever witnessed in this section closed last night at the Morrisville Methodist Episcopal Church, with an addition of twenty-eight members to the church. The meeting lasted ten days and witnessed full churches all the time. Sunday night it is estimated 750 people were present. The services were conducted by the pastor, Rev. Homer Welch, assisted by Rev. C. W. Brooks, of the Grove Baptist Church.

At recent protracted meetings at three of Rev. Mr. Welch's other churches, he had the following additions to the membership: Rock Hill, 5; Grace, 19, and Providence, 5. A total of fifty-seven, and the major portion of them adults.

FOR REUNION OF ALL VIRGINIA CAVALRY

The Powhatan Troop Put on Foot an Interesting Move.

(Special to The Times-Dispatch.)

POWHATAN, VA., Sept. 16.—The annual reunion of the Powhatan Troop Association met yesterday at Powhatan Courthouse. Captain Joseph Hobson, president; B. R. Selden, first vice-president; C. L. Mosby, second vice-president; Augustine Royal, secretary, and E. D. Hotchkiss, treasurer, all of them, old officers, were re-elected. Among those present of the old veterans were Milton McLairen, W. B. Kennon, J. Haskins Hobson, E. L. Markham, Ed. Scott, and W. S. Owen.

The ravages of time and its consequences were very plainly noticeable and the old boys realized the fact of the fast passing years.

The day was most pleasantly spent by all, but only those fully appreciate it who have had a soldier's experience. The very look of the form and face bring to memory scenes of the times that tried men's souls and bind hearts closer.

The main feature in this meeting was the adoption of a resolution and appointment of committee to confer with all other veteran cavalry associations and the veterans of this branch of the Southern army at large, looking to a grand reunion of all the veteran cavalry.

Ashland Park seemed to be the most popular and convenient place for this meeting, and for this purpose they ask the kind aid of the press.

The executive committee appointed were J. Haskins Hobson, chairman, postoffice, Belona, Va.; W. N. Kennon, Sublett, Va.; Milton McLairen, Ballsville, Va.

The Powhatan Troop was formed in 1859. Philip St. George Cocke was its first captain. It was a part of the Fourth Virginia Cavalry, Wickham's Brigade, and have a name in history worthy of the cause they loved and lost.

They have erected on the courthouse grounds a beautiful monument to the memory of this historic old company. On one side is marked Manassas, 1861; Appomattox, 1865. The silent historian for the coming generations.

Among those who attended from Richmond ...

TIED TO ... ALL ...

Old Boatman D... and Uncons... Fo...

MANY LIVES ...

The Eastern Sho... the Balance ... by the ...

(Special to The ...)

ONANCOCK, VA., ... severest storms for ... on the bay and sea... Peninsula on Wedne... blew a hurricane ro... 100 miles an hour ... telegraph and teleph... plete wreck, and the... lated from outside ... cation can be secure... stations on the seas... or the oceanside ... but it is believed to ... districts. The wind ... night blew from sout... volumes of water int... the wind changed to ... in this section be... known for years. T... Messrs. Hopkins's an... Baltimore, Chesapeak... road Company's pi... covered the wharf, ... many barrels of po... of hay and rolled a ... length of the pier ... Some damage was ... company's wharf at ... wharf and freighthou... rel factory, were wa... Wharf, near the ... Creek.

Captain Samuel ... Creek, an experience... out in the bay alone ... when the first storm ... chor at eight o'clock ... boat commence to ... rushed out of the c... wind and strong ro... when the boat capsiz... twenty miles that n... boat, and was found ... next morning at nin... conscious state.

He was brought ... now thought he will ... many boats out ye... and it is feared ma...

TAKE THE POPULAR C. & ...

TO NORFOLK, OC... HENRY AND ...

Two trains leave ... A. M. Eight hours in ... at Ocean View; ten ... and Buckroe Beach, ... at Ocean View than ...

GO TO ST... Via C. & ...

Now is the time to ... see the World's Fai... at its height and ... creasing.

C. & O. trains leav... P. M. and 10:30 P. M. ... cursions. Tickets on ...

The first part of this chapter focused on the origination of the sanatorium as the St. Albans Lutheran Boys School. However, long before it opened in 1892; members of the Powhatan, Shawnee and Cherokee Indian tribes inhabited the land on which the building now stands. The Draper's Meadow Massacre in 1775 tells the story of the horrors faced by early pioneers and of Mary Draper Ingles' journey home after her capture by the Shawnees.

The Civil War also had its share of violence on the hill overlooking the New River. In 1865 Union forces defeated Confederate forces during the battles of Newbern and Cloyd's Mountain. Union artillery bombarded the settlement of Central Depot (now the city of Radford) from the ridge where St Albans stands today.

As magnificent as the St Albans Boys School was, which is described in eloquent detail at the beginning of this chapter, it had its share of darkness. An article describing the school sums up some of the horror that plagued the intellectual students; "The atmosphere at the school was rough and competitive. It clearly favored the stronger boys (or bullies as we would say today) and made short work of the more cerebral types like one E. Blackburn Runyon, whose painful experience at the school was poignantly summed up by a yearbook editor in 1904: "E. Blackburn Runyon did not return after Christmas, much to our sorrow, as it put a stop to the football games on the terrace in which he figured prominently as the football."" Though no official records indicate that students lost their lives (by suicide or by homicide) it is rumored that several lives were lost during the time that St Albans was a boy's school.

In 1916 Dr. J.C. King converted St Albans from a boy's school to a hospital for the mentally ill and St Albans Sanatorium came into existence. Even though the treatment of mental disorders at St Albans was far superior to the care given to "lunatics" at other facilities, many patients succumbed as a result of the experimental treatments performed at this institution. Insulin Coma Therapy (ICT), Electroconvulsive Therapy (ECT) and Hydro Shock Therapy (HST) all resulted in a significant number of fatalities.

There are also several documented suicides. This obituary from the Southwest Times chronicled one such lost soul "Mrs. Susan Jane Sayers, wife of W.B. Sayers, died Saturday night at the St. Albans Sanatorium, Radford, where she had been under treatment. Her condition had been in extremis for some days and the end not unexpected, it being realized there was no hope."

Shelli Sprouse Meade

Shelli is the author of the first part of the chapter (1892-1911), *Repository of Souls: The History of St. Albans Sanatorium.* She is pictured on one of the sets from the 2015 Halloween haunted house. The theme of the spooky spectacle was *Unchained*.

On June 28, 1980 the heinous murder of Gina Renee Hall was committed not far from St Albans and her bloodstained car was found only a few hundred yards away on Hazel Hollow Road. Often, when paranormal investigations are conducted in the basement, and in particular the bowling alley, a strange and almost sentient mist is seen in conjunction with the mention of her name.

St. Albans Sanatorium is now described by many experienced paranormal teams as the "most active location on the east coast." With such a dark history it is no mystery why so much supernatural activity is recorded there.

For nearly a decade paranormal groups have investigated St Albans and the number of reports of full bodied apparitions, shadow figures, levitating objects, disembodied (often threatening) voices, physical contact , and more, are staggering.

St. Albans' most recent role as a valuable paranormal laboratory that draws investigators from around the country may not be its last incarnation. But, it will most assuredly be its most interesting.

St. Albans History – Courtesy of St. Albans Sanatorium
www.stalbans-virginia.com

CHAPTER 2
First Investigators on Scene

Mountain Ridge Paranormal Research Society

Team Founded: June 2007

Hometown: Radford, Virginia

Founders: Rachel Hodge, Jessica O'Dell, and Barry O'Dell

Team Members: Kari Surratt, Donna Surratt, Donna Martin, Debbie O'Dell, Levitt
                     O'Dell, William Russell, Chuck Thornton, Tracy Brookman,
                     Derek Lucas, and Don Hanauer, prior member and former
                     Director of Operations for St. Albans Sanatorium

Website: www.facebook.com/Mountain-Ridge-Paranormal-Research-
                     Society-204717226210741/timeline/

The Mountain Ridge Paranormal Research Society (MRPRS) has logged more hours investigating St. Albans Sanatorium (SAS) than any other group in the country. They are truly the home team.

Their first investigation of St. Albans took place in September of 2009, followed quickly by volunteer duty at the asylum in 2010. "We literally investigated from 6:00 p.m. until 6:45 a.m. that first night," said Rachel O'Dell Hodge, a co-founder of the team. "We have captured a number of electronic voice phenomena (EVPs) and other evidence, but unfortunately, the laptop that held them crashed. We lost everything!"

The first evidence of paranormal activity unearthed by the team came during that initial investigation at SAS. "We used to put our base camp at the glass doors, located as you enter into the King Center section of the building." During the course of the investigation, Barry and Jessica O'Dell, father and daughter, were at that location while everyone else was investigating. It was during this time that they began hearing the lamentation of a little girl. "The child's voice kept repeating, 'mommy, mommy,'" said Rachel.

On the same night, Barry looked down the hallway, to the left of where the base was located and saw something on the ground. He took a picture and captured an unusual purple glow. "Unfortunately, this interesting piece of evidence was one of the casualties of the laptop crash," said Rachel.

"On another day, several members of MRPRS were doing volunteer work up on the second floor near the cage area," she said. This area now features a room, which has been designed to look like a classroom. This is a feature that connects St. Albans with its first and former identity as a boy's school. Rachel continued, "I had just left to dump buckets of trash and had returned to continue cleaning. Jessica O'Dell and Kari Surratt were working with me that day and had already left the area." When Rachel walked into the room she immediately noticed that they were gone. "I turned around and stood in the hallway calling for them. As soon as the echo of my voice faded in the shadowy room, I heard a voice say, 'Do you want to play?'" Rachel, as a seasoned investigator, although startled responded, "No, thank you." She then began walking the length of the hallway and down the stairs to find her team members, feeling as if unseen eyes were watching her the entire way. She found Jessica and Kari taking a break in the cool September afternoon, outside the doors of St. Albans.

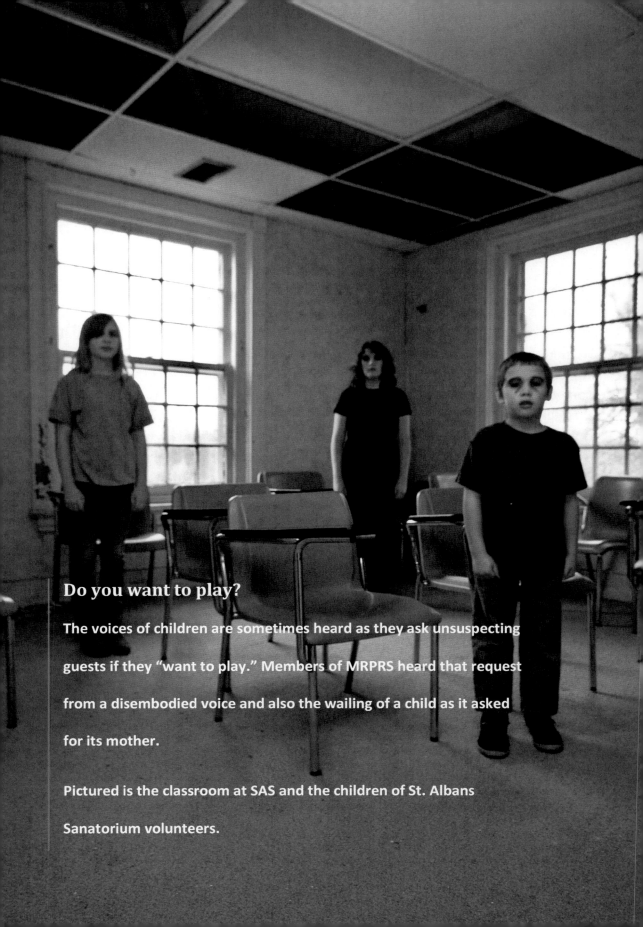

Do you want to play?

The voices of children are sometimes heard as they ask unsuspecting

guests if they "want to play." Members of MRPRS heard that request

from a disembodied voice and also the wailing of a child as it asked

for its mother.

Pictured is the classroom at SAS and the children of St. Albans

Sanatorium volunteers.

The next time Rachel experienced something paranormal in nature was some months later, during an investigation that was being recorded for radio. "At the time I was with two other people, the wife of the man who was then renting the building and another female investigator," Rachel explained. She continued, "We were down in the basement bowling alley. I was sitting on the ball return and the man's wife was sitting near the first door located as you enter into the area. At the time, the other investigator was down at the end of the bowling alley." They were busy recording an EVP session when Rachel looked up to see something that shocked and surprised her. "I saw a pair of black shadow legs move from right to left between the doors. Of course, I did not have an outward reaction until I looked for and counted my group members," said Rachel. When everyone was accounted for, she realized that she had seen a shadow figure or a ghost. Only then did she tell the others what she had seen.

Rachel isn't the only O'Dell sister to have experienced an encounter with something unusual in the night at St. Albans. "Jessica was walking a group through the building on a historical tour of the site, when she saw something that disturbed and scared her," Rachel said. "Jessica described what she saw as an 'entity with a large pumpkin head and a little body.'" One species of shadow beings that are reported worldwide are of the "pumpkin headed" variety. Exactly as Jessica described the being she saw near the grand staircase.

MRPRS crew member Chuck Thornton has had the most experiences of anyone on the team. "He has been pushed and thrown," said Rachel, recalling the ghostly abuse. "I don't remember all of the times he felt or encountered something. But, I vividly recall this one incident, because it was so intense," she said. Rachel was working with Chuck and another investigator that night to provide security for a private investigation. Two female staff volunteers had made their way into the security room, which was located near the grand staircase. "The two volunteers were cold and were trying to warm up. The activity at St. Albans was at an all-time high, with team members having some major experiences, such as things being thrown at them. Chuck, the female volunteers, the other investigator, and I were sitting by the heater also trying to warm up, when Chuck began to go into a trance-like state," said Rachel. "I noticed it and immediately began talking to him. His voice had completely changed and he began to call for his 'mommy,' in the high-pitched voice of a child," she said. Rachel then asked him where his mommy was. His voice

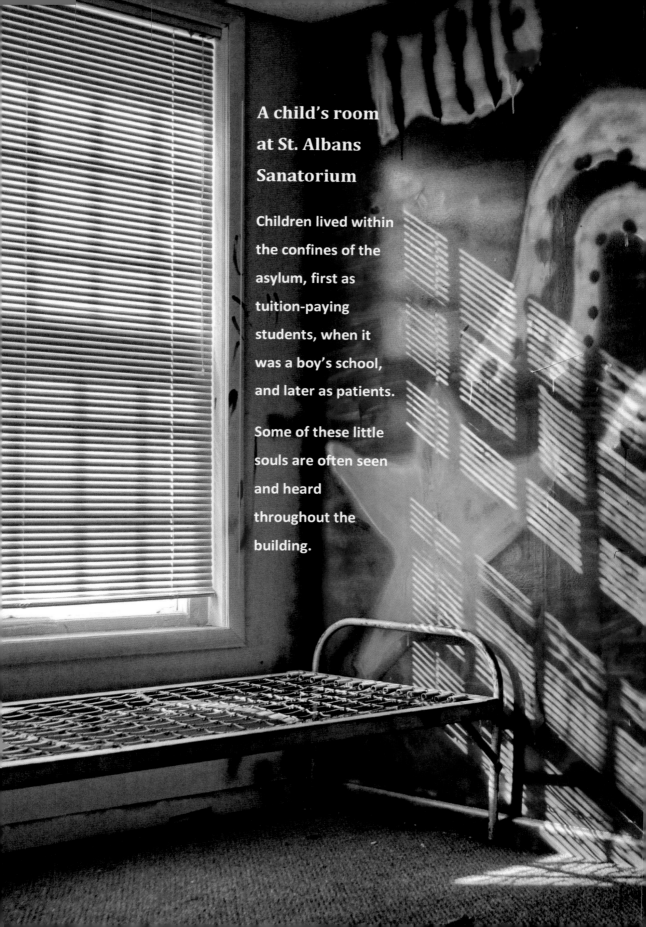

A child's room at St. Albans Sanatorium

Children lived within the confines of the asylum, first as tuition-paying students, when it was a boy's school, and later as patients.

Some of these little souls are often seen and heard throughout the building.

immediately changed into a low, raspy tone. He said, "You can't have her, she's mine." "Of course, that scared me and the other volunteers in the room. We immediately tried to wake him up," said Rachel. The women slapped him on the leg and that seemed to snap him out of it. At that moment, the other investigators in the building had moved directly above them on the second floor. Chuck suddenly said, "Don't you do it. Don't you throw that at them." Then, the other three volunteers in the room with Chuck heard a big crash and they heard an investigator ask, "What are you throwing?" Then Chuck said, "I told you not to throw it. Don't you do it again! Don't you do it!" And, again they heard a loud crash. Chuck was predicting all the times things were being thrown, as if he was connected with the unseen force in a very real way.

Even the ones who are most familiar with the secrets of St. Albans Sanatorium cannot expect to come away unscathed by her permanent residents. There is no earthly force strong enough to guard against a terrifying introduction to a ghostly and eternal inhabitant of St. Albans when she decides it's time for them to make an acquaintance.

CHAPTER 3
Recording Things That Go Bump in the Night

3:3 3 AM Paranormal

Team Founded: July 2008

Hometown: Woodbridge, Virginia

Founders: Alex and Krystal Porras

Team Members: Chuck Mandiville, Glenn Calvert, Emily Steiger, Jim
                   MacDiarmid, Austin James, Ben Stolmeir, Wade Woolwine, Lisa
                   Davis Woolwine, Ken Welscher, and Protus

Website: www.333amparanormalresearch.com

When some paranormal teams enter through the portals of St. Albans Sanatorium to investigate her dark interior, a bond is formed that calls to them, time and time again. 3:33 a.m. Paranormal is one of the teams that has heard and answered the asylum's siren call.

Led by the dynamic duo of Alex and Krystal Porras, this group of curious investigators has returned to St. Albans two or three times a year for the past six years. The team's "baker's dozen" visits to the retired sanatorium has resulted in a number of run-ins with the ghosts and entities that dwell within her hallways and rooms.

On September 18, 2010, Alex, Krystal, and Chuck Mandiville were assisting with a ghost hunting event at the closed asylum. It was during a lull in the activities of the day that they experienced a curious event. "The three of us had decided to walk around the building to take photos," said Krystal. "During this period of time the building was secured and no one was inside. Around 5:00 p.m., I was able to capture a photo, where one minute the window curtain is normal and within a second later, the curtain looks as if it is being pulled back by something unseen."

Later that night, the investigators were with Mountain Ridge Paranormal Research Society (MRPRS) members Chuck Thornton and Barry O'Dell, who were assisting the sanatorium on the ghost hunt. "We were on the second floor in Jacob's room, when we heard something out in the hall. We all proceeded to get up and take a look. The atmosphere in the area was very heavy, as if someone was sitting on my chest," said Krystal. At that moment Chuck began acting unusual, as if something was bothering him on an emotional level. "Suddenly, he began telling something that none of us could see to, 'back off.'" She continued, "It was as if Chuck was being assaulted. We all heard an audible growl within the room, responding exactly to his energetic attempt to push the entity off of him. During Chuck's tussle with his unseen assailant, which took place around 11:00 p.m., I took photos of him and not one of the pictures were in focus." According to Krystal, her camera was capable of taking photos in low light situations and she had taken photos both before and after the event that were perfectly in focus.

Barely a year later, team members were once again face-to-face with the darker Denizens of the old sanatorium. "In October of 2010, we held a public

Encountering spirit energy

The number of encounters that investigators from the 3:33 a.m.
Paranormal and Appalachee Paranormal teams experienced at St. Albans
is not surprising, considering the number of tortured souls caught within
her grasp.

Pictured is the room where a grieving, but insane mother was allowed to
keep her deceased baby, in a jar in the closet.

investigation with fellow ghost hunters, Matt Cline and Jeff Griffith from Appalachee Paranormal. We split the participants up into small groups of ten each and each team leader took them to separate areas of the building," said Krystal. The team leaders were careful to make sure that each sub-team was in a distinctly separate part of the building so that any evidence captured would not be contaminated by other people in the building. "The first portion of our investigation had me take them to the basement, electroshock therapy, and the hallways leading up to what is known as the dragon room," she said. "The group I was leading was comprised of female Radford University students. As we were walking down the long hallway, the girls became upset when they had their shirts tugged by unseen hands." When the group arrived at the bowling alley area of St. Albans, the makeshift team experienced cold chills and heard knocking. But, the most unsettling experience was yet to come. "The most intense moment of the night took place in the bowling alley," said Krystal. They had set up for an EVP session when an anomaly occurred that could not be ignored. "Suddenly, we all heard growling. This thing proceeded to go from girl-to-girl, growling at them. It caused them to get very upset and I had to end the session early."

Two years later on September 3, 2012, 3:33 a.m. Paranormal had arranged for Friar Bob Bailey to present a teaching event for interested paranormal investigators. "This was the date of the most hostile experience I have had there," said Krystal. After the lecture, there was an investigation in which Jeff and Matt from Appalachee Paranormal joined, Alex, Chuck, and Krystal to explore the building.

The members of Appalachee Paranormal were using an application on their phone that night, which acted as a ghost box. A ghost, spirit, or Frank's box is a radio that has been modified to scan stations. It is thought that a spirit can manipulate the device to communicate with investigators. On this night, the ghost box application started saying and spelling out, "Krystal Porras, I've been a bad boy," repeating itself several times. Matt then decided to use the PSB7, another type of ghost box, which uses radio frequency sweeps to generate white noise through which, theoretically, ghost voices can be heard, and it proceeded to say the same thing. Concerned, Matt then took out the PX box (this device has a 2,000 word vocabulary programmed into the box and, theoretically, a spirit can manipulate the device to communicate) and to no one's surprise there that evening, began repeating the same thing.

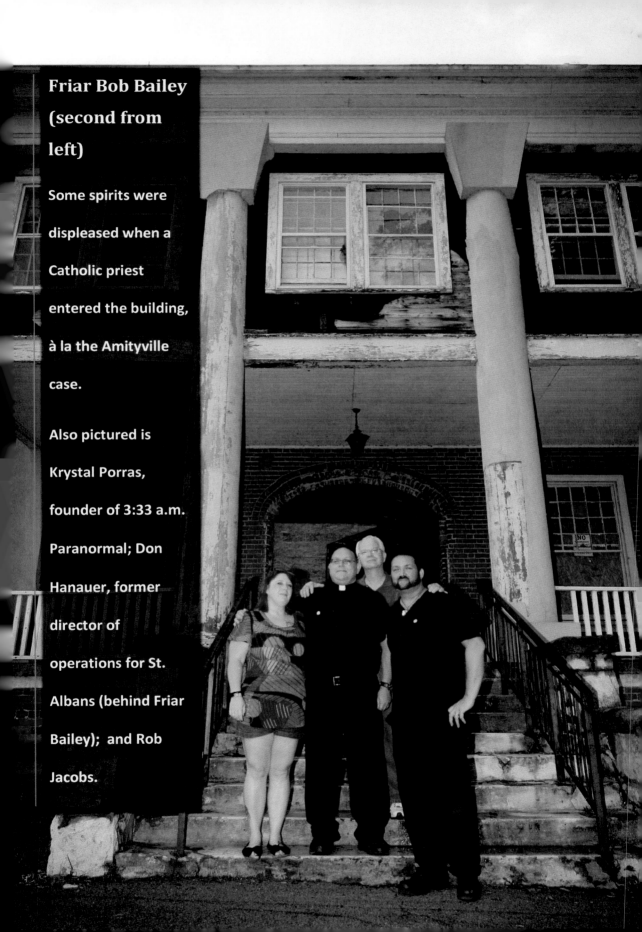

Friar Bob Bailey (second from left)

Some spirits were displeased when a Catholic priest entered the building, à la the Amityville case.

Also pictured is Krystal Porras, founder of 3:33 a.m. Paranormal; Don Hanauer, former director of operations for St. Albans (behind Friar Bailey); and Rob Jacobs.

"Once we moved into a room off of the dragon room, the messages became very hostile stating, 'you wh*res, I'm going to hurt you' and my favorite, 'I'll kill you,'" said Krystal. "I have investigated St. Albans many times and I am used to the spirits calling my name, but this was the first time I ever had them say my first and last name together. It took me a while to figure it out, but I remembered an important detail. At the end of Friar Bailey's lecture, he said over the intercom, 'I would like to give a special thanks to Krystal Porras and St. Albans for putting this event together.' I guess the spirits did not like the fact that I brought a Catholic Priest into the building who played a mock deliverance over the intercom," explained Krystal.

Later that night, the team moved into the bowling alley and activity began to escalate. Appalachee Paranormal members Jeff and Matt began using Cross Over Talk. According to the website, www.crossovertalk.com, "Cross Over Talk is an online interface to an experimental instrumental trans-commmunication (ITC) device." "I had never used this before. I swear, it is like a direct line to Hell," said Krystal. "This very strange soft voice began to speak, it was almost like one of those creepy voices in a movie. It would respond to our conversation." The room began to reek of rotting flesh and the stench made team members feel as if they would regurgitate. "I actually stated that, 'I feel like I could vomit, this smell is horrible.' This eerie, raspy voice came over the radio responding to my statement about becoming sick, 'goooooood.' The tension in the room built until it really felt like something was going to attack. We felt threatened so we decided to wrap up the investigation prematurely,'" she said.

The team of 3:33 a.m. Paranormal is well acquainted with the ghosts and entities of St. Albans Sanatorium. They know that the building is a repository for a wealth of paranormal activity. Some of this activity and ghosts are benign, while others are nefarious in nature. She is a mixed bag, this old asylum. St. Albans' very nature cautions the investigator, both timid and bold to, "tread carefully, all ye who enter here."

CHAPTER 4
Connecting with the Dead

Southeast Virginia Paranormal Investigations

Founded:	June 2010
Hometown:	Newport News, VA
Founders:	Clint Griffith, Todd Spangler, and Adam Bridwell
Lead Videographer:	Rick Hutson
Website:	www.virginia-paranormal.com

Southeast Virginia Paranormal Investigations (SVPI) is led by Clint Griffith, Todd Spangler, and Adam Bridwell. One other member, Rick Hutson, rounds out this band of supernatural sleuths. These four paranormal investigators are known for their fearless pursuit of all things preternatural in nature. They are also recognized throughout the field for their ability to develop or tweak technology to aid them in their hunt for supernatural activity.

In addition to arguably having more contacts with the ghosts and creatures that inhabit St. Albans Sanatorium in the fewest visits, SVPI is also known for the episodic documentary, <u>Paranormal Apprentice</u>, which was created by their production company, Para-Fright Productions. On May 26, 2012 the team arrived on the doorstep of St. Albans Sanatorium with the intention of filming for the documentary. The evidence they gathered during this visit was phenomenal and plentiful.

"From the second I set eyes on the old abandoned sanatorium on the hillside in Radford, Virginia, I knew my squad and I were in for a night full of experiences," said Adam. "Our team usually unloads all of the gear on the grounds prior to walking into any location, but for this particular site I think we were all so anxious to just step inside for the first time." SVPI investigators were enthralled by St. Albans as soon as they crossed the threshold of the building and felt her energetic welcome. "I could literally feel both the positive and negative energies that reside at St. Albans Sanatorium. The temperature drop upon entering the building was significant, at least 15 to 20 degrees Fahrenheit. I knew right then that the energy inside St. Albans Sanatorium was alive and it was apparent because it greeted us at the door," Adam said.

Fellow SVPI Co-founder Todd Spangler agreed with Adam's assessment of St. Albans, "We caught an overwhelming amount of evidence from the moment we set foot in the place, filming b-roll footage in broad daylight. While Rick (Hutson) was walking through the sanatorium, he caught EVPs (electronic voice phenomena) of sinister laughing and what sounded like multiple spirits talking about us. The first spirit said, 'tonight is the night,' followed by the second spirit that said, 'all f*cked in the head.'" Rick also heard a doorknob turn and the creaking of a door opening directly behind him. Startled, Rick

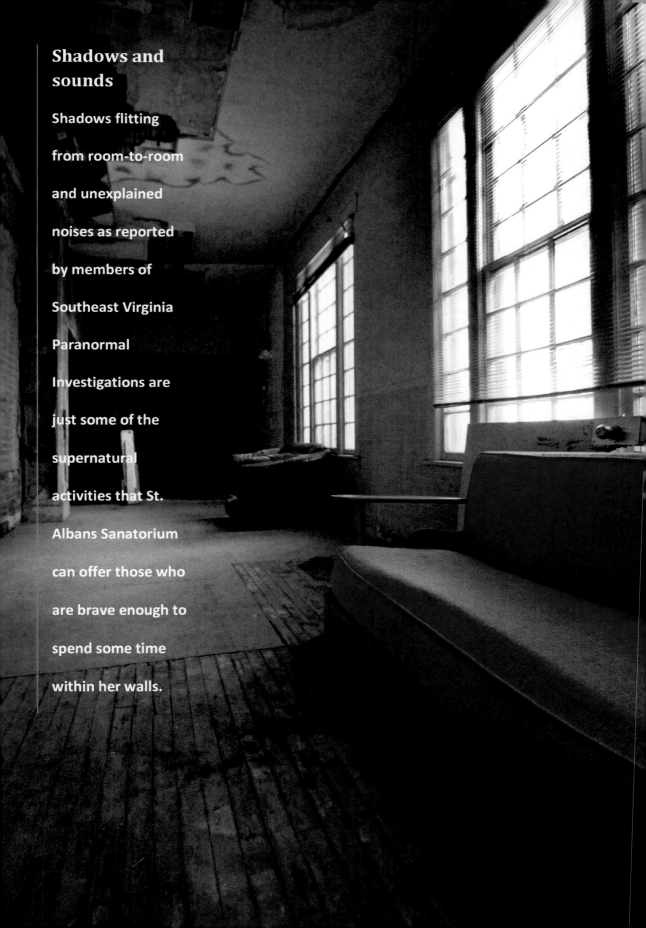

Shadows and sounds

Shadows flitting from room-to-room and unexplained noises as reported by members of Southeast Virginia Paranormal Investigations are just some of the supernatural activities that St. Albans Sanatorium can offer those who are brave enough to spend some time within her walls.

swung around and saw . . .nothing. The door behind him was closed and didn't even have a doorknob attached.

This was just to be the beginning of the paranormal activity that assaulted the members of SVPI during that visit. Even before they began their investigation, a static camera they had set up in the electroshock therapy room started to record evidence. "We began seeing what appeared to be fog on the camera," said Todd. He continued, "Two of the investigators ran down to see what it was and as they entered the room, the fog seemed to change direction quickly and disappear." They continued to see the fog as the camera recorded for almost the entire night. The only time that the "fog" appeared was when no one was in the room. Later, during an investigation session in the electroshock therapy room and after they had used the Jacob's ladder (also known as a Tesla ball, a device by which it is thought that spirit energy can manipulate static electricity), they captured the fog on camera, which appeared in the room to the right of the investigators. It then moved quickly out of the doorway. "We researched the development of fog in interior spaces and found nothing scientifically that could substantiate what we were seeing on our infrared night vision camera that evening," said Todd. "The fog moved intelligently, we could not see it with our own eyes, and it seemed to avoid human contact."

One of the team's favorite technological tools is the SB7 and the SB11 Spirit Boxes. "The journey these devices took us on that night, from the suicide bathroom to the second floor hallway is one of the most impressionable moments of my life," said Todd. That is a bold statement, as Todd has been investigating the paranormal since he was six years old. In all those years, he has not made a connection with a spirit as he has with what they call the "Tongue Man" at St. Albans.

"Our investigation session started on the third floor in the area of the suicide bathroom. I started an EVP session in the bathroom as I sat on the edge of the tub," said Todd. "Not two minutes into the session and I began feeling ill to the point of wanting to throw up." He decided to leave the bathroom and sat just outside of the door, requesting that Adam (Bridwell) go sit in the bathroom to see if he could experience the same sick feeling he had felt. "While I was in the restroom, we heard a disembodied voice of a female answer one of my questions," said Adam. "I asked, 'Did you kill yourself in this bathroom' and the voice replied, 'Yes, I did.'"

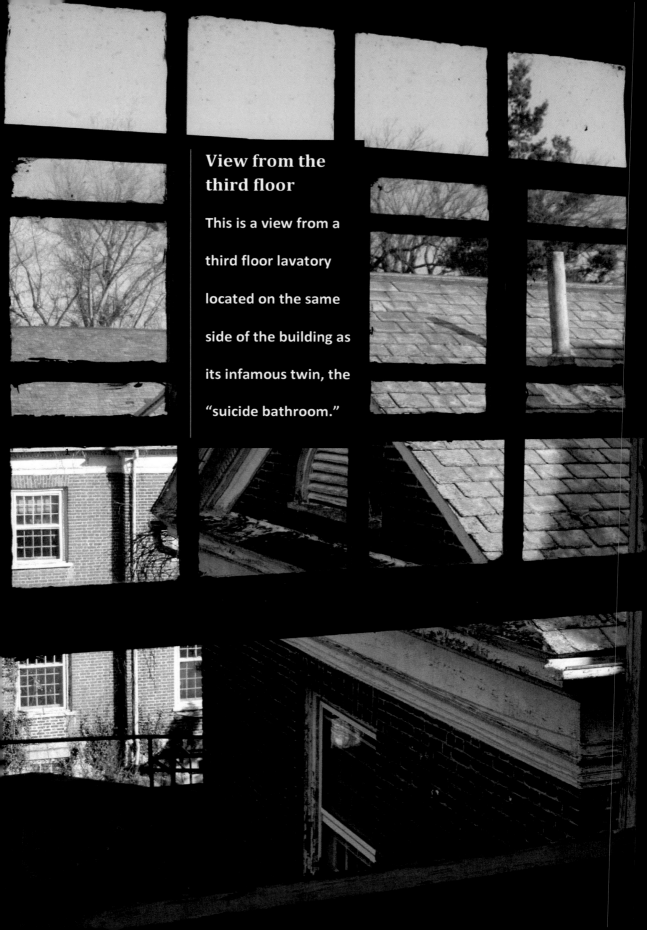

View from the third floor

This is a view from a third floor lavatory located on the same side of the building as its infamous twin, the "suicide bathroom."

The team, which that night included Stephanie Spangler, Todd's wife, caught the response very faintly on their DVR audio. "We started the SB7 Spirit Box shortly after that and began asking questions," said Todd. The following is a transcript of some of the questions and responses the team received from the session, starting in the suicide bathroom and then as they moved throughout the third floor and up and down the second floor hallway:

Adam: "Are you still here with us?"
Female SB7 response: "maybe"

Adam: "How many are here with us right now?"
Male SB7 response: "eighteen"

Adam: "Are you in pain?"
Male SB7 response: "I'm in pain."

Adam: "Can you tell me your name?"
Male SB7 response: "The Devil."

Todd: "Do you want help?"
Male SB7 response: "You'll help us do it."

Adam: "Tell us why you're still here."
Male SB7 response: "The Devil."

Todd: "Are there any males present with us right now?"
Male SB7 response: "He died here."

Stephanie: "It's much colder in here."
Male SB7 response: "Open up the door."

Adam: "Are you touching me or trying to touch me?"
Male SB7 response: "I did." "Let Adam speak....Adam"

Todd: "Did you just call Adam's name?"
Male SB7 response: "I did."

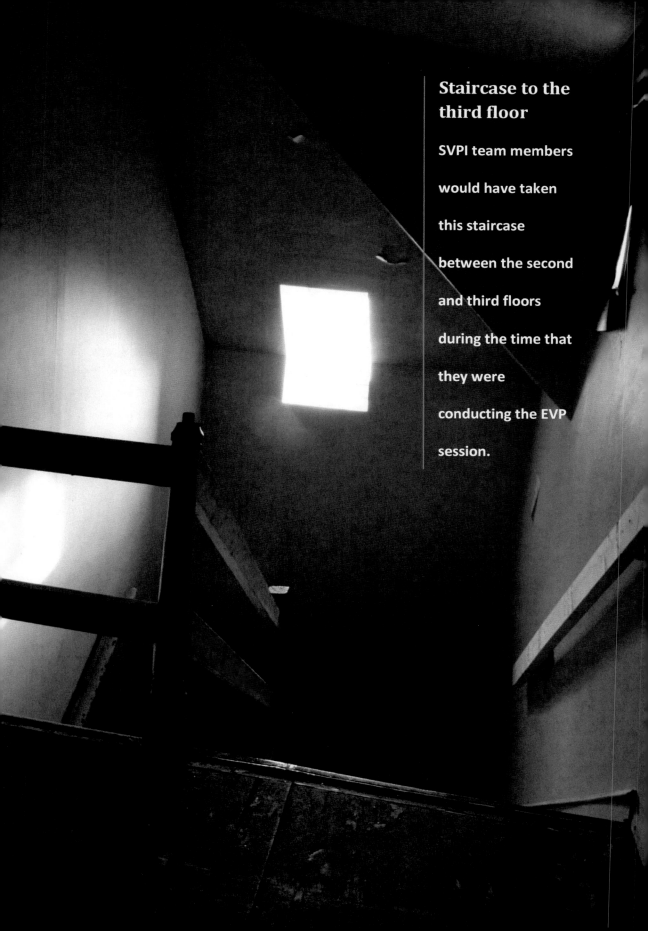

Staircase to the third floor

SVPI team members

would have taken

this staircase

between the second

and third floors

during the time that

they were

conducting the EVP

session.

Adam: "What's the gentleman's name in the middle of the room?"
Female SB7 response: "Todd," "honey" (This is the nickname that Todd's
wife Stephanie calls him.)

As the team departed the third floor for the second floor, they received
an instruction that came through the SB7 from a male spirit who Todd now
recognizes as the Tongue Man, "Look up." This response became highly
significant as they ventured down the second floor hallway.

"We walked down the second floor hallway from one end to the other
not getting any credible or intelligent responses over the SB7. We turned
around to do one last sweep of the hallway and adjoining rooms and then end
the investigative session. Even though it was pitch dark on the interior of SAS,
as we were approaching the stairwell area I could faintly see something to the
top left out of the corner of my eye. I looked up to see what it was as I did not
want to hit my head on anything. That's when it showed himself to me. From
the top of the doorway a face popped out and startled me. I jumped back
saying, 'Jesus f*cking' and a response on the SB7 said 'The Devil,'" recalled
Todd. At the same time this happened, Adam received a spike of EMF
(electromagnetic field reading) on the MEL meter (a piece of equipment built
specifically for ghost hunters).

Suddenly, Todd saw something that he will carry with him for a lifetime.
"I saw the Tongue Man clearly, however, only the front half of this face was
visible. The way it projected itself was like seeing someone come through a
pitch black portal into a focused light source, which caused the face to glow. It
had no hair and sunken eye sockets with no eyes, and its jaw was elongated
and mouth open farther than is humanly possible," said Todd. After regaining
his composure in a minute or two, he went in pursuit of the being.

As the group continued down the hall of the second floor asking the
Tongue Man questions, Todd made a request for the creature to "talk to me
through this device," referring to the SB7. "What happened next has never
happened to us before. In response to my request, the SB7 Spirit Box actually
cut itself off. Then, a man's voice came through it saying 'I did' and then the SB7
cut itself back on. This was the first time we've experienced anything like this
through one of our devices. The premise of the SB7 is to allow the spirits to
speak through white noise, however this was not how the device reacted in this
case. Unusual reactions by electronics have happened to the team since that
time at SAS, but only there and in the presence of Tongue Man."

EVP Session

Clint Griffith of SVPI is shown leading an EVP session in the electroshock therapy room at St. Albans Sanatorium.

These were some of the responses that the team recorded as the night progressed:

Male SB7 response: "I know how to speak." (Received, but not in response to an immediate question.)

Female SB7 response: "Todd"

Male SB7 response: "Where's the baby?" (It seemed like these two spirits were trying to communicate with Todd, but not in response to a question.) We believe the baby that was being referred to was the progeny of the woman who stayed on the third floor whose child was premature and still born."

Todd: "Stop hiding."
Male SB7 response: "I am and I love it."

With the last response, SVPI decided to wrap up the session. "My heart was pounding as quickly as it had when I was a child and I had seen an apparition that startled me," said Todd. He continued, "This was the beginning of my relationship with Tongue Man. During our next two visits to SAS he responded to me through knocking, footsteps, and through his favorite means of communication, the SB7. However, I've never captured an EVP using my digital recorder that I could definitely conclude was him."

All of the above mentioned ghostly responses can be found in Episode I of The Paranormal Apprentice. The trailer for the episode can be viewed here, http://paranormalapprenticetv.com/.

The next time SVPI returned to St. Albans was on November 16 and 17, 2013 for a 36-hour lockdown. "We were filming again for an episode of Paranormal Apprentice and came prepared for a very long and very cold stay at SAS. The amount of evidence captured on the trip was no surprise considering what we experienced our first trip," said Todd.

The first contact made was with the Tongue Man in the bowling alley. As the team conducted an EVP session, they began to get intelligent responses by loud knocking. It didn't take the team long to find out it was the spirit. "The knocks were so loud and prominent, like he was excited that someone knew who he was. I began asking questions about him and his physical appearance," said Todd. He continued, "Tongue Man claimed to be misunderstood and

Engineering SVPI Equipment

SVPI's Adam Bridwell is pictured preparing equipment at the team's base camp in the King Center before an investigation at St. Albans Sanatorium. The team is known for engineering equipment to their specifications.

that he could not help the way he looked. It was at this point that I really started to feel an emotional bond with him. I felt sorry for him because not only was he a patient at SAS, he was a patient who was an outcast even among the ranks of the insane. He claimed he did not mean to scare people, but he understood the way he looked. He also remembered me and how he scared me on the second floor from our first visit. From the first time we made contact, I never felt threatened by him."

During another investigative session on the second floor, Todd was using the SB7 Spirit box and literally had a real time conversation with Tongue Man. "He said he wanted to play a game, so I went along as he took the team and me on a hunt for him going from the suicide bathroom all the way down to the file room and back up to the second floor. He would give us clues over the SB7 like 'purple room' or directions like 'down' and 'behind you.'" The team remembered the 45 minutes as a unique ghost chase, in which the ghost gave clues for them to follow. They never found him. "Eventually, he just stopped responding, which puzzled me. On another SB7 session on the second floor later in the 36 hour investigation I found out that there was something much more sinister at SAS and Tongue Man was scared of him or it," said Todd.

The rest of the SVPI team traveled to the second floor, because they wanted to experience what Todd did earlier in the evening by contacting the Tongue Man through the SB7. "For some reason we could not make contact with him through the device immediately as we have in the past. What sticks out in my mind was when, over the SB7 the words 'Todd, stop' came through. I had the feeling of a heavy presence there, unlike the normal energy of the Tongue Man. I respected the response and turned off the SB7. Immediately after that we captured a class A EVP with two voices," said Todd. The first was very deep and said "Let's GO!!" and the second voice who Todd believed to be Tongue man said, "Let me go!" After hearing this EVP and hearing the warning over the SB7 Todd knew that this was the spirit warning him that someone or something else was there that could endanger them. "Quite frequently at locations we capture evidence indicating that there is one entity or spirit, which presides over all of the other entities and/or spirits at the location. SAS does not appear to be any different. It's almost like the spirits are not supposed to communicate with our world and if they get caught they get punished. While conducting an active EVP session we heard, 'he's coming' and all communication stopped, which leads me to believe there may be overseers," said Todd.

On an investigation of St. Albans

Todd Spangler of SVPI is shown during an investigation of the fabled sanatorium. He is pictured leading an investigation in the "classroom" on the second floor.

The final, significant experience members of SVPI had on this trip was when they tried to get a couple of hours of shut-eye. "It was very cold, so we had hung tarps over the doorways to this room on the first floor where we decided to set up our base camp. We had a portable heater running, but it was still extremely cold. I was leaning against the doorway next to one of the tarps. We had all of our gear boxes and bags sitting just outside the room. I couldn't get comfortable so I wasn't getting any sleep. I began to hear shuffling outside the doorway and what sounded like someone rustling through our bags. Clint, Adam, and Rick were asleep so I decided to take a peak because I thought it was Stephanie or the apprentice who elected to sleep in the truck," said Todd. When he checked, there was no one there. He continued to try and get some sleep, but by this time the sun was already starting to come up and he knew it was a lost cause. "I began hearing the rustling outside the doorway again, so this time I grabbed my DVR camera and went out. Again, there was no one there. I traveled down the hallway where I was hearing noises and circled through a room to the opposite doorway to our base camp. This particular doorway had two tarps attached to it; one taped to either side of the door jam and was not used as an egress. Everything seemed to be in order and I found no one roaming about so I concluded it was just some curious spirits wondering what our bags contained," said Todd. He returned to the other doorway and entered the base camp where he continued to try to get some rest. "Not three minutes after I got settled back down, a loud noise came from the tarp hanging on the doorway right next to me. The tarp was a heavy green poly material that contained a ridged pattern. The sound appeared to be a fingernail starting at the top of the tarp and running all the way down to the bottom, creating an almost zipper like sound. It was so loud it woke up Adam and Clint," said Todd. The three of them looked at each other, grabbed their gear and headed out to investigate.

They roamed the halls for a while, getting no responses on their recorders, giving up, they headed back to base camp. As they approached, they heard a commotion and found that the inside tarp had fallen onto Rick and he was struggling to throw it off of him. Rick told the team that he had heard a noise and then the tarp fell. "I circled around to the outside of the doorway to investigate," said Todd. He continued, "The exterior tarp was still up, but had an impression in the middle of it like someone punched at the tarp. I had just gone over to that side of the doorway, not an hour earlier and the tarp was perfectly flat and taped down as it should be.

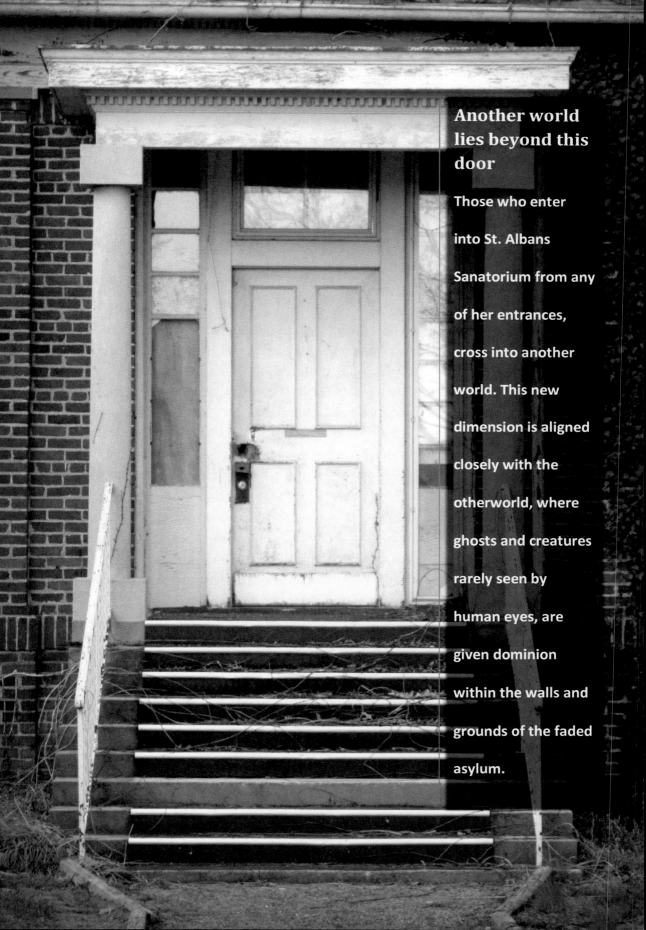

Another world lies beyond this door

Those who enter into St. Albans Sanatorium from any of her entrances, cross into another world. This new dimension is aligned closely with the otherworld, where ghosts and creatures rarely seen by human eyes, are given dominion within the walls and grounds of the faded asylum.

"Did a spirit punch the tarps from the outside, causing the inside tarp to fall on Rick? Based on the occurrences throughout the night, I would claim yes," said Todd.

This evidence and more, is slated to appear in <u>Paranormal Apprentice</u>, Episode 3, *Return to St. Albans.*

On August 24, 2014, SVPI hosted a number of individuals for an investigation of the sanatorium drawing seasoned investigators and novices alike. Although others, including Stephanie Bussard of The Ghost Writers, and a reporter, had substantial experiences, such as encountering shadow figures, SVPI members did not. It well could have been that those with the SVPI team were too engaged in leading groups on investigations throughout the building to tune into the ghostly energy themselves.

Clint Griffith, one of the cofounders of SVPI described the reporter's experience. "During the investigation that evening, we used the Jacob's ladder for about 15 minutes and witnessed it interacting directly with us. The male reporter who was covering the event that night, identified himself at the beginning of the investigation as a total skeptic," said Clint. The reporter left St. Albans the next morning with a totally different mindset. "I asked him to hold a para-corder, an instrument that picks up on electricity and also gives off its own energy source. The reporter proceeded to tell us that he heard a breath right beside him and knew no one was in close proximity. When the reporter said, that was 'really weird,' the para-corder started going off as if it was picking up on some anomaly nearby." The incident changed the reporter from a skeptic to a believer in the existence of paranormal activity.

In the corporeal world, we connect with other living souls. These people have completed our lives as friends and relatives. Perhaps the kind of connection that SVPI and the Denizens of the asylum have developed is an otherworldly friendship forged by the energy that is St. Albans Sanatorium.

CHAPTER 5
Personal Experiences at St Albans

Bedford Paranormal

Team Founded: January 2007

Hometown: Bedford, Virginia

Founder: Alan May

Team Members: Scott Detamore, Ronnie Anderson, William Ondell,
                  and Kiley Revis

Website: www.bedfordparanormal.com

Bedford Paranormal founder, Alan May, has a close connection with St. Albans Sanatorium. Long before he first led his team into the murky, twilight of the building, he had called on her four different times. Alan investigated the building on several occasions with another team of preternatural sleuths from Radford, Virginia that sent an invitation for him to join them for a public investigation.

"Back then, the building was in much rougher shape before the current management team took over and made the building much safer," said Alan. "On my first investigation of St. Albans, as we walked the halls getting a feel for the layout of the building, I could see spent shell casings on the floor and graffiti, courtesy of local teens. These individuals entered the building at times to explore and to have a place to hang out. I wondered if any would enter and interfere with our recordings later that night. None did though," said Alan.

From the evidence left behind, it looked like some of them had climbed the fire escapes on the outside of the building and entered from the top of the building. There were also several cats living in the building at the time, but they were quiet and wild enough to stay out of sight.

Although Alan did not get any evidence on voice recorders or cameras during these initial investigations, he did have a couple of personal experiences. "On one occasion, we had set up a base station in a couple of the rooms right off of the glass doors to the King Center," said Alan. He continued, "There was a hallway to the left and a long one directly ahead. Several people were convinced that they could look down the long hallway and see a dark shape peering out of rooms momentarily and then ducking back out of sight," he said recalling the incident.

His second experience with those who live permanently within the walls of St. Albans involved the disembodied footsteps of someone whose physical presence was long gone, but whose spirit remained within the sanatorium's cold embrace.

On this investigation, Alan had been part of a larger group, which was then split up into smaller teams. He and his newly formed band of paranormal investigators walked to the far end of the building, on the second floor. At that juncture, there were a couple of hallways and a fenced-in patio.

King Center

NO
TRESPASSING
Violators
will be
prosecuted!

The King Center

The newest section of the structure that comprises St. Albans Sanatorium is the King Center. Within these walls, many sightings of paranormal activity are reported.

"My group decided it would be a good location for an EVP session, so we set up in one of the rooms and started asking questions. We made the usual inquiries that most groups do, and I also asked if anyone needed help or needed to pass on a message to a family member," said Alan. About a half hour later, the entire group heard what seemed to be footsteps walking down the hall. There were no other teams or individuals in that area at the time of the observation. In addition, since their room was at the end of one of the halls, at least two of them could see down the hallway. Anyone coming up the steps from the floor below would have been visible to them, at least momentarily. "We listened for a few minutes and decided it might be a homeless person or a teen walking around, so we left our room and searched the floor, only to find . . . nothing," he said.

At that point, they decided to try investigating elsewhere in the building. "We walked down the stairs, standing near the landing for a few minutes," said Alan. He continued, "A couple of people were talking when we again heard footsteps. They seemed to come from the second floor area that we had just left. We looked at each other silently as we listened. As quietly as we could, we went back up to the second floor, but no one was in sight. Again we searched the rooms and again we found them empty. Although we didn't gather any audio or visual evidence, it was a good personal experience."

A few years later, Alan took his team, Bedford Paranormal, which included Ronnie Anderson, Scott Detamore, and William Ondell to hear a presentation on the history of the building. The talk included information about its residents, those that had worked there, and the transformation of the building from boys' school, through its incarnation as a sanatorium, and into its final guise as a world-class location of paranormal repute. "We were able to talk with other investigators that we hadn't seen in a while, hearing of their experiences and learning about the building. We toured the building and the first thing I noticed was how much safer it was." The management team and volunteers that were taking care of it had improved the structure. Where he once felt that the floors might give way at some point, they now felt solid and well-built. "It was easy to see that they cared about the building and those that investigated it by improving the structure, but not changing the look or feel of the beautiful Victorian era architecture."

Sometimes, as Alan and his team found out, the ghosts of St. Albans Sanatorium refuse to reveal themselves to modern devices, preferring to reach out directly to those who reach out to them. Anyone interested in exploring this

Shadow People

A number of reports have been made by paranormal investigators who have encountered shadow people within the dark recesses of St. Albans Sanatorium. Bedford Paranormal is one of the teams whose members were introduced to the inhabitants of the obsolete madhouse.

magnificent location with the intent of making contact with the souls within her walls should use caution. When someone crosses the threshold of the portal into her domain, she and she alone will determine whether your stay is like a cloudy dream or the darkest nightmare. The mistress of the phantoms within is an enigma that is not prone to accept disrespect lightly.

CHAPTER 6
No Fear of the Dead

VIPER Paranormal

Team Founded: October 2008

Hometown: Roanoke, VA

Founders: Mike St.Clair and Amanda Mattox

Team Members: Dale Justice, Bryan Mattox, Lisa Martin, Chris Martin,
                   Amanda Shockey, and James Rogers

Website: www.viperparanormal.com

The team members of VIPER Paranormal are what could be termed, "frequent flyers," at St. Albans Sanatorium (SAS). They have visited her cool interior in their capacity as supernatural detectives more than 15 times.

On November 12, 2011, during a TAPs Academy (The Atlantic Paranormal Society, of "Ghost Hunters" fame), they encountered a rather noisy ghost; a phantom that certainly did not want to be ignored.

That night, Amanda Mattox, co-founder of VIPER Paranormal, Angie Cline, of VIPER WV, and Ken Kestner, who at the time was with Michigan Ghost Runners, set out on their own to explore the dark rooms of the old asylum. "We ended up in the isolation rooms where the women were held, during the time St. Albans served as a sanatorium," said Amanda. "Angie was standing near the door to the bathroom and Ken was setting up video near the back of the room. I was setting up my recorder near the windows in the same location. As we were having a discussion about the nurses needing a bulletproof window to protect them, we heard a really loud and distinct noise," she said. Amanda continued, "It sounded like someone kicked the wall near Angie. It startled her so badly that she ran across the room!" In the style of dedicated paranormal investigators everywhere, each time Amanda goes back to St. Albans, she makes it a point to visit the site of this hostile encounter.

While investigating on a later date with Angie Cline and Don Hanauer, the former Director of Operations for St. Albans, the team saw shadows darting from door to door. They also heard a bell, but felt that bit of information could be discredited on the fact that it could have been something hitting a piece of metal in the building.

St. Albans Sanatorium was again in rare form on March 24, 2012. On that date, Bryan Mattox, James Rogers, Mike St.Clair, and Amanda Mattox heard crying emanating from deep within the core of the now defunct asylum. The piteous sound can be heard on the YouTube Channel "screamfreak79" at https://www.youtube.com/watch?v=F6yB_nZBgOQ. The title of the video is, *Screaming Ghost Caught on Tape?" St. Albans Sanatorium!* According to their YouTube site, the team believes that it may be the screams and crying of, "a former patient who may have been tormented by unimaginable acts once believed to cure a wide variety of mental ailments." Indeed, the early science of psychiatry was fraught with archaic and torturous treatments.

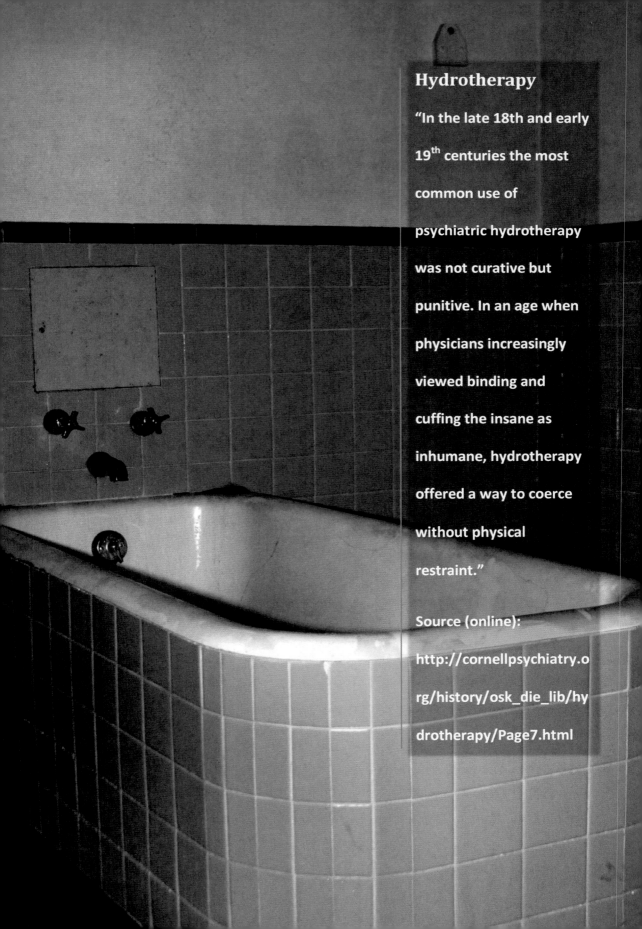

Hydrotherapy

"In the late 18th and early 19th centuries the most common use of psychiatric hydrotherapy was not curative but punitive. In an age when physicians increasingly viewed binding and cuffing the insane as inhumane, hydrotherapy offered a way to coerce without physical restraint."

Source (online): http://cornellpsychiatry.org/history/osk_die_lib/hydrotherapy/Page7.html

Patients would be subjected to a number of possible cures, while held within an asylum. Among the most barbaric of these treatments was the use of Trephination, which is boring holes in the head. Practitioners thought that by doing this, it would relieve pressure on the brain and in turn, heal the sick mind. This curative is thought to have started as a remedy for mental illness as long as 7,000 years ago. It is believed that trephination may have been a practice aimed at eliminating or reducing headache pain, or relieve the mind, so that mental recuperation could take place.

Bringing possible psychiatric treatments into the Victorian era, asylums were often overcrowded affairs. Families would not only bring their mentally ill members for treatment, but also to remove them from the household. Having a family member who had a mental illness cast an unsavory reputation on everyone sharing the same household. Asylums often became storehouses for the helplessly insane.

The 18th century was replete with adventurously misguided treatments for those who needed psychiatric help. At that time, physicians had not separated mental and physical ailments. They felt that both must be connected in some way. As a result, physical tortures were prescribed for the unlucky patient. Ice water baths, where the patient was held helplessly immobile while immersed in icy liquid was often prescribed. This dated cure-all was supposed to shock the mind back into perfect working order.

Physical restraints and isolation were also items on the early psychiatrist's, "let's try this and see how it works list." But, from the darkness of those earliest days of dramatic trial and error have come the much more successful treatments of today.

At the time the members of VIPER Paranormal recorded the former patient screaming endlessly into the night, the team was all accounted for and located on the second floor, above what is now known as the purple room. The sound itself seemed to permeate from some distance inside the sanatorium.

Sounds of frustration and terror are part and parcel of this grand and venerable structure. It is the music that breaks the quiet of the night, suddenly and without warning. These echoes of sounds through the ages are reminders of the people who left impressions upon the very fabric of time and space. Reminders ripped from the pain and agony of the person into the cloth of the location known as St. Albans Sanatorium.

CHAPTER 7
Seeking Evidence of the Afterlife

7 Cities Paranormal

Team Founded: April 2013

Hometown: Newport News, Virginia

Founders: Scott Spangler, Tim Hoover, and Sherry Baier

Team Members: Sarah Mitchell, Bandon Schaefer,
Larry Baier, Heather Moore, and Wayne Lincoln

Website: www.7citiesparanormal.com

There are shadowy creatures that survive within the walls and rooms of St. Albans Sanatorium, according to Scott Spangler, co-founder of the team, 7Cities Paranormal. "I've encountered shadow beings on several occasions at St. Albans, including a run-in with what we call the creeper and the hat man," he said.

7Cities Paranormal was founded by Scott, Tim Hoover, and Sherry Baier in 2013. This is the third team that Scott has either founded or served with in the dozen or so years since he began seeking answers to "what comes after death" in the supernatural realm. He is known throughout the paranormal community as an active and serious investigator.

During a late afternoon in 2011, Scott was unloading equipment with a member of a former team to which he belonged. The two men were standing inside, near the riverside door situated on the far right of St. Albans, when Scott noticed an unusual dark figure at the end of the hallway. "We were standing to the left side of the grand staircase when I saw this figure, which appeared to walk straight out of the wall," said Scott. The being was described by the investigator as being, "blacker than black." "It was moving back and forth across the hallway on all fours, when suddenly, the creature swung its head in my direction, as if it saw me staring back at it," he said. Although Scott couldn't see the face of the being, he felt its intense gaze. The shadow being froze in its exodus for just a few seconds as the investigator and entity stared transfixed at each other. Then, it turned and ran, disappearing into another wall.

Unfortunately, on this visit, Scott was unable to overtake and confront the strange shadow figure. But, he would encounter the strange being again, the next meeting would also introduce another shadow creature, The Hat Man.

Scott visited St. Albans Sanatorium an additional two times during the years from 2011 until his next encounter with the shadow creature, which took place on May 2014. It was on this third subsequent visit that he was reintroduced to the creeper. He and his teammates from 7Cities Paranormal had traveled from Norfolk to Radford, Virginia to investigate the infamous sanatorium.

"My team members, Lori, Sarah, and Jenny (Jones, a former member), were in Jacob's room upstairs about 2:00 a.m., trying to communicate with the

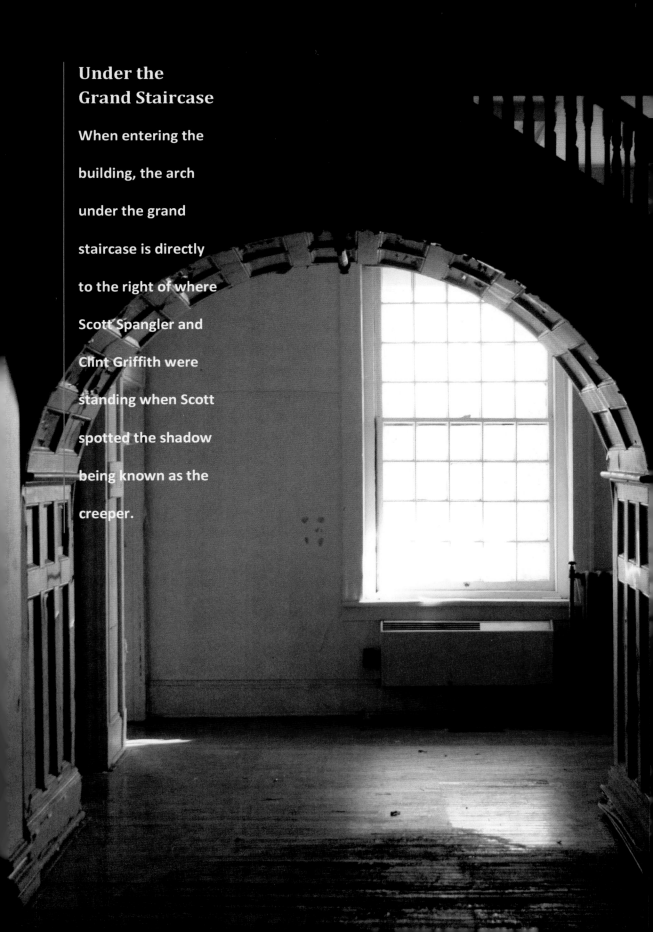

Under the Grand Staircase

When entering the building, the arch under the grand staircase is directly to the right of where Scott Spangler and Clint Griffith were standing when Scott spotted the shadow being known as the creeper.

spirit of the boy," said Scott. "Jenny saw Jacob behind Sarah, near the wall that is next to the open door. Jenny said that she felt warm and really good and for a second, she thought it was Jacob," he said. The euphoric feeling would not last.

Suddenly, Jenny felt dread. She turned to look in the direction where she felt something staring at her and was face-to-face with the creeper. The creature had peeked its head out from behind the door, only a few feet from her. It was on all fours and, according to Jenny, its head was oblong and ugly. In addition, its arms were abnormally long and spindly.

The creeper stared at her, its head cocked in an unnatural position, as if it could spin its odd shaped noggin' in a 360 degree rotation, like the girl in the movie, The Exorcist. Jenny got up to close the door, but to her horror, the creeper had moved inside the room with her. It then fled into a dark corner of the room before disappearing before her terrified eyes.

"I was outside at the time this happened," said Scott. Fortunately for him, a team member immediately came out and told him that they had seen something that was exactly like the creature Scott had described from his earlier visit to St. Albans.

"I grabbed my flashlight and ran up the steps. I said, 'I know you're here. I've seen you before.' I heard something creeping down the hallway trying to make an escape to the other side of the second floor." What he heard were not footsteps, but something skittering down the hallway, banging into the walls as it fled the investigator, who was in determined pursuit.

"My thought as I began chasing after the shadow being was, 'This isn't happening,'" said Scott. But it was, and the strange interaction was quickly unfolding. This kind of supernatural activity is why investigators go into places with a paranormal reputation, so that they can try to find answers to the great mysteries of life and death.

He continued on his hunt of the being. "I was excited, as in pumped from adrenaline, and immediately ran up the hallway to catch up with the shadow being," said Scott. He heard someone shout at him to stop, but he was so focused on connecting with the being, that the warning seemed like muffled, background noise.

Even though Scott's flashlight was on, the creeper blended so totally into the blackness of the shadows and darkness of the hallway, that he could not see the creature. "I couldn't see it, but I could hear it as it ran," said Scott. He called out to the creature, "Show yourself. Show yourself to me!" Scott ran after the creeper until he found himself alone and in the center of the left-hand

Stairs to the second floor

These are the stairs to the second floor via the grand staircase. Jacob's room is to the left of the landing. Members of 7Cities Paranormal took this route to the location where they captured a voice on an audio recorder saying, "look behind you."

wing of the second floor, where the elevators are located. Suddenly, a strange figure stepped out of the shadows and walked purposefully across the hallway directly in front of Scott.

"This shadow figure was very tall, no shorter than six feet two inches in height. It was dressed in a fedora-style hat, and a long coat and didn't seem to be perturbed at all that I was there," said Scott. The shadowy figure paused for just a second and then casually continued his walk, only to disappear into the wall. "This thing had an authoritative bearing, like he was someone who gave orders. The creeper was more like a pet; it was a scaredy cat that ran like a frightened animal. I could tell the Hat Man wasn't afraid of me, but I wasn't afraid of him either," said Scott. His only regret is that he was unable to make verbal contact with the Hat Man before the being dissolved completely into the wall.

Although those were the only two times that Scott and his team members have come in direct contact with the creeper and the Hat Man, it is not the only time that they have gathered evidence of paranormal activity at SAS.

In 2012, about 4:00 p.m. on a November afternoon, Scott and Tim Hoover were in St. Albans doing a walkthrough of the building. At the time, they were the only two on the property. They were around the corner, near Jacob's room when they were discussing some exposed pipes. Scott said, "Bet that's not working anymore." A spirit answered in a whisper, "Look behind you."

Evidence, including the EVP just mentioned that was gathered at St. Albans and at other locations 7Cities Paranormal has investigated, can be found online at www.7citiesparanormal.com/our-evidence.html.

Why are some people, like Scott and others who don the mantel of paranormal investigator, drawn to the dark embrace of the sanatorium? It may well be the case that the answer lies in the fact that their thirst for evidence of the otherworld is never so quenched as at that fountain of paranormal activity, St. Albans Sanatorium.

CHAPTER 8
Walking Through the Veil

HAUNT Paranormal

Team Founded:	June 2005
Hometown:	Abingdon, Virginia
Founders:	Jennifer Woodward-Proffitt, Adrienne Harless, and Ashley Sturgill
Team Members:	Michael Proffitt, Eddie McCowan, Kevin McCauley, Alexis Harless, Lee Cox, Shanna Coleman, and Anthony Coleman
Website:	www.hauntparanormal.com

HAUNT Paranormal (Hunting and Understanding National Terrors) was founded by three women, Jennifer Woodward-Proffitt, Adrienne Harless, and Ashley Sturgill on June 13, 2005. Since then, these fearless females have led their team of paranormal investigators through St. Albans on several occasions.

It was on one of these visits that several members of the team were witness to the manifestation of a shadow person. This anomaly presented itself on the first floor of the building, near the women's isolation ward.

"The team had just left the men's ward and we were getting ready to set up our cameras when I thought I saw something out of the corner of my eye," said Jennifer. "When I turned around to see what it was, my team members followed my line of sight."

"When I saw Jennifer looking towards the door, at first I didn't notice anything," said Adrienne. "But once my eyes adjusted, the dark shadow became crystal clear and it was a silhouette of a man who was leaning against the door frame."

"I was with Eddie McCowan, another team member and we both witnessed the presence of the shadow man," said Ashley Sturgill, one of the team co-founders. She continued, "We called for the remaining two investigators who were there that night and who were located just a few rooms down the hallway. When they heard us call, Shanna and Anthony Coleman came running into the room. Shanna immediately noticed the dark outline of a man."

On that same investigation, when they came to the top floor, near the suicide bathroom, Adrienne began having an unexpected feeling of despair. At the time she had no idea where the infamous paranormal hotspots were located in the building. "Eddie had researched St. Albans before we left," said Adrienne. She continued, "After I told him of the overwhelming sensation of sadness I was experiencing, Eddie mentioned that there was a bathroom located on the floor that we were on that was known to have been the site of several suicides." Adrienne then asked one of the sanatorium's volunteers Sarah Sanders, and was told that they were standing next to the infamous bathroom.

Near the suicide bathroom

Scene from the third floor of the sanatorium, where the HAUNT Paranormal team member felt the overwhelming sense of despair. This location is near the infamous suicide bathroom, where several patients ended their tortured lives.

Pictured are props from a fundraising event.

This was not the only paranormal encounter experienced by these investigators that night. Eddie, Anthony, and Lee Cox were standing in what is known as the cage (also, the birdcage), an outside porch covered with wire. When the sanatorium was operating, this location was used to allow the living tortured souls of the asylum an opportunity to breathe fresh air and feel the sun's rays flicking off their pale skin.

"I felt like I had been hit by an energetic hammer," said Eddie describing the intense incident that was seared into his memory that night. "I immediately looked towards the dark doorway and saw a huge bright blue light hovering in the blackness." He continued, "The light was roundish, not round and seemed to be moving down the hallway towards us. Before I could grab my camera and take a photo, the light faded before our eyes." Two other team members bore witness to that anomaly, Anthony and Lee were also looking in the direction of the supernatural ball of light.

Jennifer overheard Eddie, Anthony, and Lee's exclamations about the blue orb. "We immediately came to their location with cameras in hand," said Jennifer. Like Eddie, they were too late to be able to capture visual evidence of this anomaly. It is theorized that orbs of this type may be a manifestation of spirit energy.

The final, significant incident that this team encountered at St. Albans came during a later investigation. Jennifer, being a dynamic investigator broke her own team's rules and ventured solo onto the second floor. While there, she investigated what is known as "Donald's room." This is the room in which an alleged paedophiliac orderly resided who was accused of murdering a small boy, known as Jacob. The story goes that the little boy was found dead in his bed and no autopsy or follow-up was ordered.

Jennifer was in the room by herself for about 20 minutes before a manifestation by the child-ghost occurred. "I felt a presence there, but initially wasn't able to define where the energy was located," she said. "I had my camera in my hand scouring the room to try to connect with this spirit, when all of a sudden I felt a small hand on my back pushing me on the upper hip." She continued, "It wasn't a hard shove, it was a gentle push, as if all Jacob wanted was for me to step out of his way."

"I was very excited to experience this paranormal activity," said Jennifer. "I saw Pat Bussard O'Keefe coming up the stairs to the second floor landing. I immediately asked her to come into the room and to stand about 18 inches from the wall on the right side of the hallway doorframe.

Jacob makes contact

Beneath this text is a photo of the wall where the little boy-ghost known as Jacob made contact with Jennifer Woodward Proffitt of HAUNT Paranormal and Pat Bussard O'Keefe, the author and founder of The Ghost Writers. The photo was shot from inside Donald's room.

"It was an exciting encounter," said Pat, "we, as paranormal investigators spend hours on end tracking possible paranormal anomalies and to have something this profound happen is memorable." When Jennifer asked her to step into the room, Pat immediately told her not to tell her what she may experience inside. She wanted her mind to be clear and free of any possible suggestions. "I stood next to the wall for about three minutes, when suddenly a small hand from the ether reached out to push me out of his way. It was a gentle push by a tiny hand on the small of the back. This child meant no harm, but only wanted his space," she said.

St. Albans is known to welcome ghost hunters with a plethora of paranormal activity, if a team is lucky and the energy is right. Shadow people, active orbs, a child's ghost, and the reports of disembodied voices, ghosts of all ilks, entities, and more that are reported by others in this book are just part and parcel of this magnificent haunted structure. Entering through the door of St. Albans Sanatorium is easy, it's what you find there that may cost you just a little bit. . .of your sanity.

A drawing of Jacob, by artist and medium Christine Downes. Drawing courtesy of St. Albans Sanatorium.

CHAPTER 9
Investigating the Great Mystery

NEAR: North Eastern Anomalys Research

Team Founded: March 2009

Hometown: Staten Island, New York

Founder: Bruce Wayne Barraclough, Jr.

Team Members: John Cronin

Website: www.facebook.com/NEAR2010?fref=ts

Bruce Wayne Barraclough, Jr., is the founder and director of a team that, like many, have been called to St. Albans Sanatorium to make a connection with the immortal spirits that walk within her walls. Upon his arrival, he felt so connected to the ethereal essence of the asylum, that he and his team later went on to develop an event designed for the sole purpose of helping to reconstruct the wood, stone, and rock of the sanatorium back into its original form.

"*Paranormal Restore* was a conference that brought together leaders in the paranormal field who wanted to help save St. Albans," said Bruce. "They gave presentations and workshops for a number of interested individuals, many of them paranormal investigators. It was followed by an expedition to meet the spirits of the old place."

"I and the rest of my team of NEAR: North Eastern Anomalous Research have been to St. Albans Sanatorium on several occasions, working on projects to help keep her alive, in a very real sense," said Bruce. One of the projects of which they are most proud is the restoration of the magnificent grand staircase.

St. Albans drew Bruce to her, as she has many of the investigators and others mentioned throughout this book. But, for some, the meeting with her can be intense and strangely personal. For Bruce, the greeting included a special kind of welcome wagon.

"There were so many times that I have experienced supernatural phenomena at St. Albans," said Bruce. "It is one of the most actively haunted places I have ever investigated." This makes a statement as Bruce has investigated dozens of sites, all of which have been reported as rife with preternatural disturbances.

His first encounter with an otherworldly resident at the sanatorium took place on a night when the shimmer of a full moon lit everything with a silvery sheen. That evening, he and another team member entered St. Albans through the King Center. Before entering the building, he noted that there was a disturbance in the weather and that a thunderstorm was fast approaching.

An increase in paranormal activity is often noted during the onset of a storm, as if the increased energy in the air can invigorate a spirit. This, in theory, makes them stronger and better able to manifest paranormal activity.

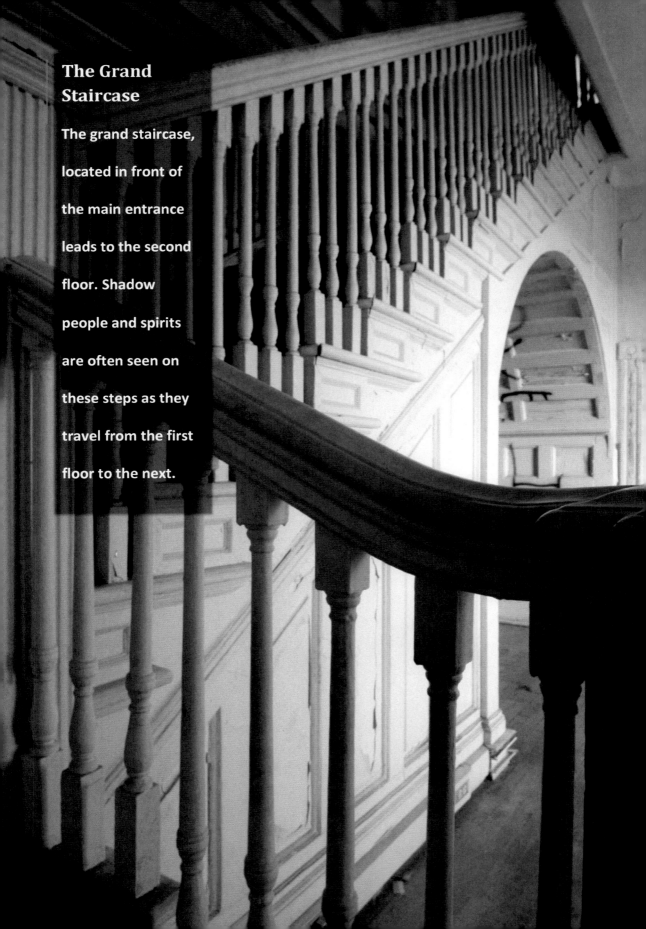

The Grand Staircase

The grand staircase, located in front of the main entrance leads to the second floor. Shadow people and spirits are often seen on these steps as they travel from the first floor to the next.

"The energy was so surreal that you could actually feel the difference from right outside the Center's doors until you took that first step inside," said Bruce. The two supernatural sleuths wondered through the dimly lit hallways for a couple of hours until they stopped in the purple room. At that time they set up and began an EVP (electronic voice phenomena) session. It was a little later during this period of the investigation that they took out the full-spectrum digital camera. "We began to feel the hairs go up on the back of our necks and it was at that moment that we knew we were not alone," said Bruce.

Approximately a half-hour later they continued on their way back towards the grand staircase; when they arrived at their destination, Bruce moved towards the left of his team member and began taking photographs of him as he sat on a step of the grand staircase. "About 20 minutes into the session, we started smelling a bad odor. Imagine smelling a corpse that had been freshly laid out in a morgue, it was that disturbing," said Bruce. He continued, "Suddenly, I heard a loud knocking sound that came directly from behind us. I began taking a quick succession of photographs and was interrupted by a deep, powerful voice telling us to 'get out.'" To respect the request of the Spirit that had asked them to remove themselves from the premises, they left and returned to the St. Albans Inn, where they were staying that night.

"When we began going over evidence, we looked at our photographs and discovered what appears to be the shadow of a little boy in the purple room. I showed the photo to Marcelle Hanauer, who is the director of operations for St. Albans, and she shared with me the story of a child's spirit named Jacob," said Bruce. Jacob is the spirit of a little boy who was rumored to be murdered during the time St. Albans served as a sanatorium. Jacob is thought to wander throughout the asylum but, is most reported in "his" room on the second floor. The location of Jacob's room is part of the wing that served as the children's ward at the time.

The two investigators continued culling through the over 700 photographs they had taken during their investigation that night, looking for additional visual anomalies. They were not disappointed. They found a photograph of what appeared to be someone in a long dress or long shorts. Both Bruce and his team member were wearing jeans that night. "I am hesitant to say for certain that this is a definitive photograph of a spirit," said Bruce. "It well could have been a camera glitch, but it is an interesting photograph, nonetheless."

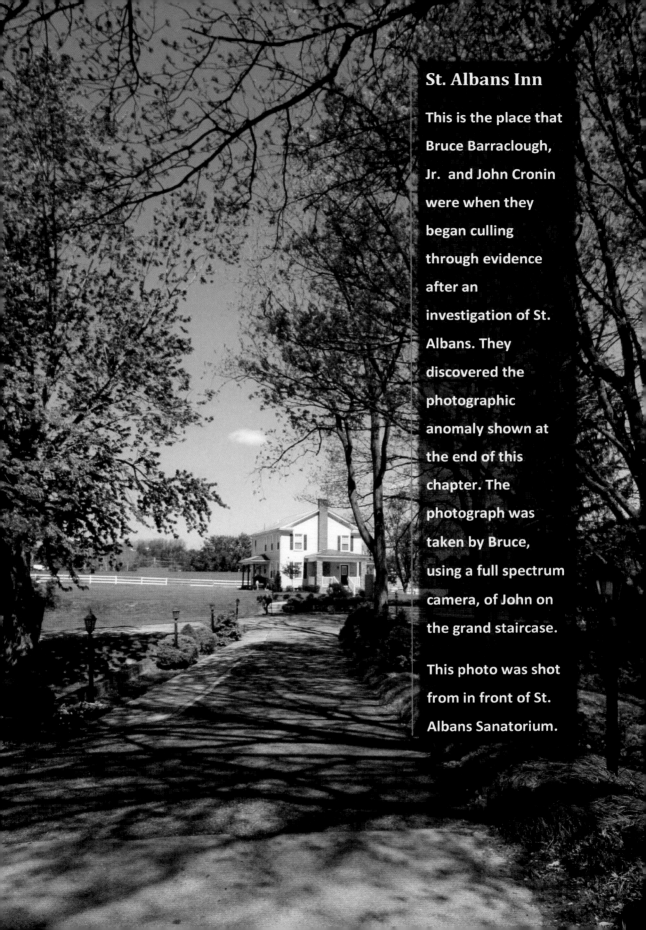

St. Albans Inn

This is the place that Bruce Barraclough, Jr. and John Cronin were when they began culling through evidence after an investigation of St. Albans. They discovered the photographic anomaly shown at the end of this chapter. The photograph was taken by Bruce, using a full spectrum camera, of John on the grand staircase.

This photo was shot from in front of St. Albans Sanatorium.

Bruce is one of the individuals that St. Albans has energetically grasped to her cold bosom. As part of the favoritism she has shown him, she has opened the once closed door between the living and the dead and has introduced him to some of the many spirits she holds captive.

"I have heard the screams of a woman coming from isolation. I can no longer go into what is called the 'dragon room,' because when I do, I become sick. At one time, we were in the birdcage (also known as "the cage") when a door knob came flying at us," he said. The birdcage is the rooftop room, surrounded by wire mesh,
designed as a place for the sick of body and mind to safely enjoy the sun and moon. Bruce continued, "Chuck Thornton, head of security for SAS, was with us when we were near the electroshock therapy room and experienced a light bulb being thrown so forcefully that it flew over our heads all the way to the other end of the long hallway."

His introductions to the former patients and staff of the asylum are plentiful. "At another time, I was near the grand staircase with a volunteer from St. Albans doing an EVP session and trying out the Ovilus, when about ten minutes into the session we felt we had negative energy around us. We then smelled something like wood burning and had the physical sensation of breathing it in. Suddenly, the Ovilus said 'Burn Henry outside.' The connection was too obvious to be ignored."

An Ovilus is a device used by some paranormal investigators that is supposed to convert environmental readings into words. There is a theory that spirits are able to manipulate these factors in order to use the Ovilus to communicate.

Bruce and the team of NEAR not only love the incorporeal being that is St. Albans, but they respect her. When St. Albans Sanatorium takes a liking to someone she becomes like a rich and decadent addiction. Each visit is as strange and delightful as the first, making her beloved crave just one more sojourn into the shadows of her soul.

Strange Image

Look at the photo

directly below this

text. Is the anomaly

caused by slow shutter

speed, or is it a spirit

caught on camera?

Photograph courtesy of Bruce Barraclough, Jr.

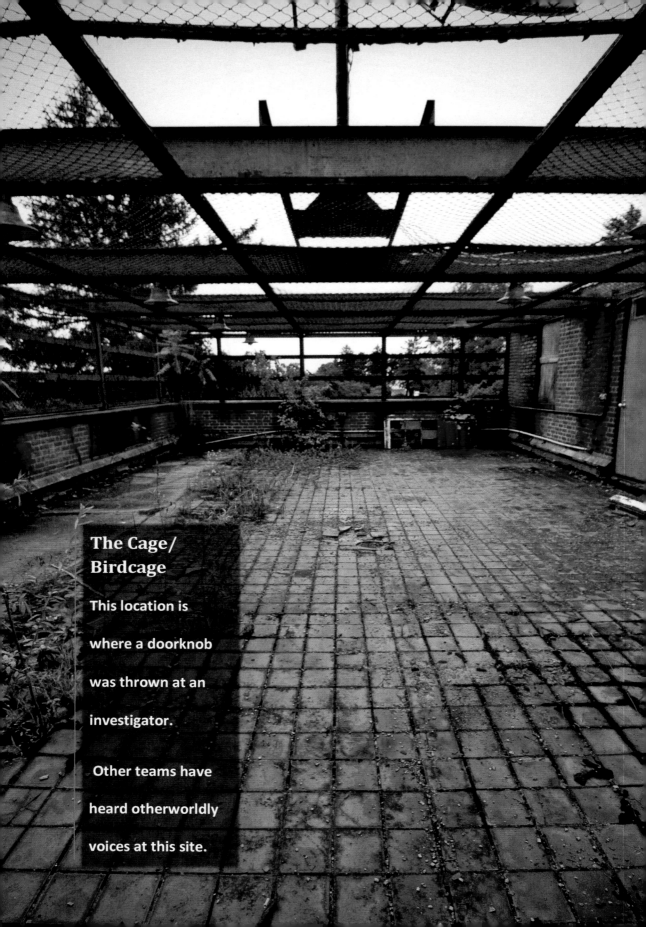

The Cage/ Birdcage

This location is where a doorknob was thrown at an investigator.

Other teams have heard otherworldly voices at this site.

Chapter 10
Experiencing the Unexplainable

Sisters of Salem
Society of Paranormal Research (S.O.S.)

Founded: August 2011

Hometown: Salem, Virginia

Founders: Ashley Conner, Rachael Ross, and Misty Conner

Team Members: Taylor Nicole Wyatt-Hill, Nicole LaPrade, and
                    Shanna L. Presnell

Website: www.sistersofsalem.com

The Sisters of Salem Society of Paranormal Research, better known as the Sisters, or S.O.S., is an all-female team that knows when to have a good time and when to get serious on an investigation. Their infectious good humor and zeal for the paranormal field is well known in what is a very small community of preternatural investigators.

The Sisters have visited St. Albans on a number of occasions. In addition to private and public investigations, members of the team have volunteered for the Sanatorium's fund raising attractions. Their initial encounter with the grand old lady was on August 20, 2011. On that night the three founders, Misty Conner, Rachael Ross, and Ashley Conner were becoming closely acquainted for the first time with a structure that would open the door to a tempest of paranormal activity.

Their first private investigation at the sanatorium was made possible because another group of investigators from Florida had setup an investigation and extended an invitation for S.O.S. to join them. Amelia Island Paranormal and East Tennessee Paranormal Research Society were two of the groups with whom they inspected the rooms and hallways of St. Albans for evidence of a haunting. They were not disappointed.

"Jeff, who was the founder of Amelia Island Paranormal, had to evacuate St. Albans shortly after the investigation began because he could not breathe when he went into the 'Dragon' room,'" said Ashley Conner. She continued, "He reported that he felt as if he was being choked. Unfortunately, someone had broken into the room before our investigation and spray painted symbols that were believed to be Satanic. After Jeff's attack, sanatorium volunteers painted over the symbols and it seemed to ease the energy in the location. You can imagine how this would set the tone for our investigation."

Ashley's sister and teammate also had a significant experience at St. Albans that night. Misty found herself alone in the electroshock room. Seasoned paranormal investigators always travel in no fewer than pairs when inspecting a location. Misty was aware of that rule, but had become separated from her team. At the time, S.O.S. was a new group of supernatural enthusiasts. The frightening encounter Misty had while in the bowels of the building was a lesson that shook her to her core. Her experience has made the team

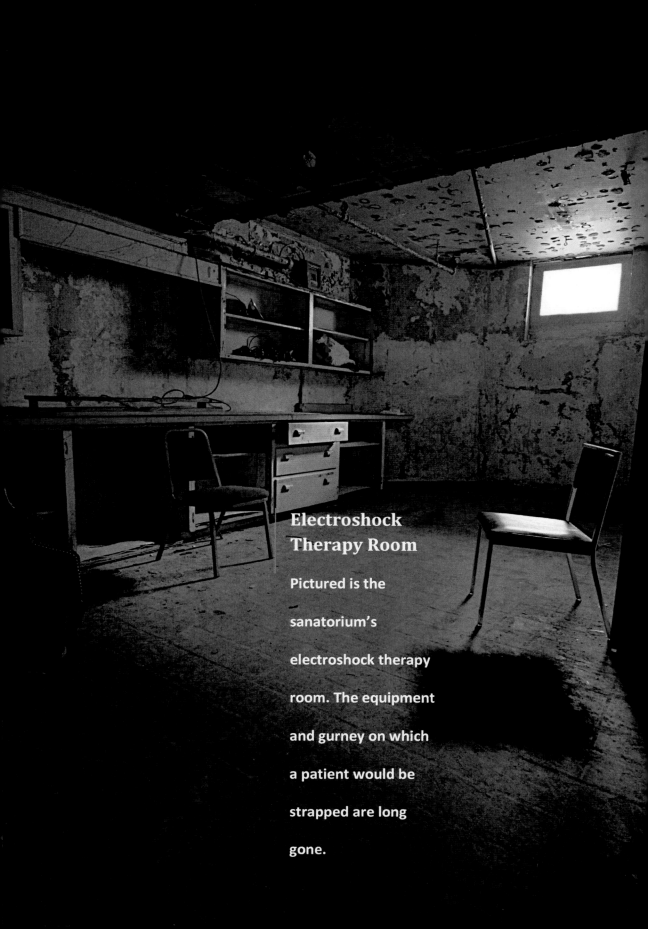

Electroshock Therapy Room

Pictured is the

sanatorium's

electroshock therapy

room. The equipment

and gurney on which

a patient would be

strapped are long

gone.

hyper-aware of the need to partner when investigating a reputedly haunted location.

"I was waiting for a part of my team to emerge from phlebotomy, while the other part of the team went down to the bowling alley. I realized at that point that I was all alone standing at the threshold of electroshock, at the entrance to the long hallway," said Misty. At that moment of realization, she heard a noise. "I turned my flashlight on and pointed it towards the sound, which was coming from the pipe above me and what I saw shocked and confused me at the same time," she said. What she saw was paint peeling off a pipe. Not a small piece, but a large portion of the paint was being pulled away from the pipe in a slow, deliberate motion. "There was no one there except me and me alone," said Misty.

Terror flicked up her spine and traced itself to the nape of her neck. "A feeling of fear came over me, and when I say fear, it was such an intense feeling of fright that I have only felt this at one other location in my investigating career and that was at another very active place, Old South Pittsburg Hospital." OSPH as the hospital is known in ghost hunting circles is located in South Pittsburg, Tennessee. Misty felt that whatever was there that night manifesting through the physical act of pulling paint off a pipe wanted to frighten her.

When Misty found herself alone in the electroshock room, she realized that she had broken a cardinal rule of paranormal investigating. She knew she should have stayed with a partner for the length of the investigation.

After the incident, when audio and video was culled for traces of evidence, the team found a clear EVP. "The audio clip sounded like 'run for it' or 'run Forest.' The movie Forrest Gump was released in 1994 when St. Albans was still used to warehouse the addicted and mentally ill," Misty said.

The Sisters of Salem have discussed a possible experiment, playing the movie in one of the active rooms in St. Albans to try to trigger a response from the wraith. Investigators such as famed Electronic Voice Phenomena expert Michael Esposito have pioneered similar experiments with varying degrees of success.

Another connection to the movie is that Ashley had been quoting Forrest Gump all evening. "I had actually asked her to stop quoting it," said Misty. Another theory could be that the Spirit heard the sisters discussing the movie and in an attempt to communicate, used the phrase, "Forrest Grump." Auditory "catches" are common at the old sanatorium. On another night, S.O.S was investigating with the seasoned team, East Tennessee Paranormal

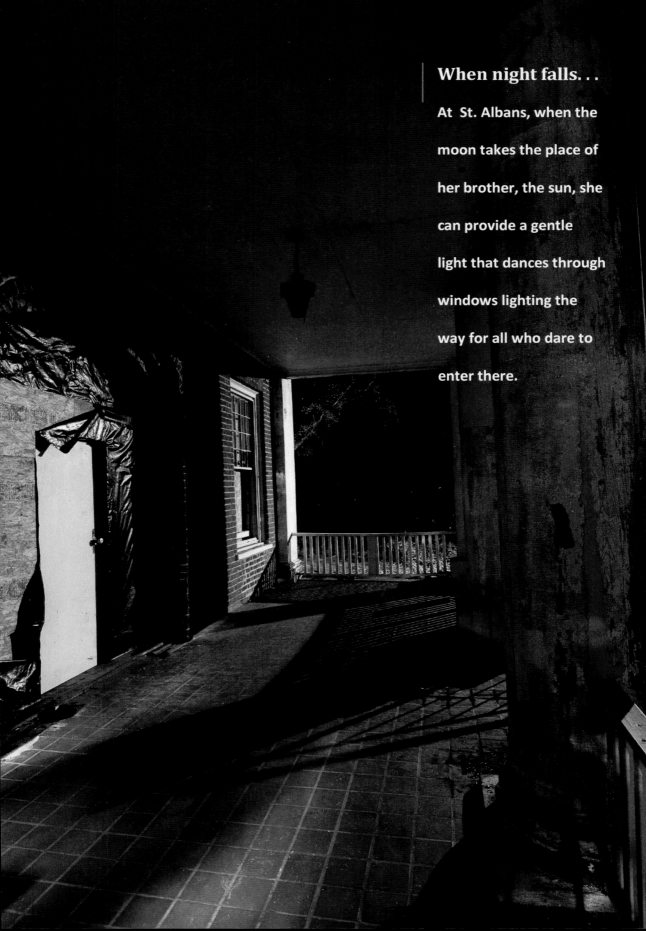

When night falls. . .

At St. Albans, when the moon takes the place of her brother, the sun, she can provide a gentle light that dances through windows lighting the way for all who dare to enter there.

Research Society (ETPRS). ETPRS used an Ovilous while on the joint investigation. An Ovilus is an instrument created by former electronics engineer Bill Chappell. The device in essence, measures changes in environmental energy fields and modulates those changes into audible speech using a synthesizer chip, an English word vocabulary, and a technical function that sounds out words.

During this investigation the Ovilus was used extensively and kept repeating the same name over and over, Peter. "The name Peter was phonetically sounded consistently by the Ovilus," said Misty. The name was repeated so frequently that they ignored it and assumed it was a glitch. The incident was forgotten soon after the investigation ended.

A few months later, S.O.S. founders Misty, Ashley and Rachael Ross attended another paranormal event and as they were talking with members of another team they were surprised by what they heard. "They informed us that they had also investigated St. Albans and one thing that stood out to them on their investigation was a disembodied voice that was heard at the grand staircase," said Misty. A name was manifested so loudly by a spirit so that everyone in the room could hear it clearly. The name was Peter. The team completed extensive research after the recording, which had taken place three to four years before they spoke with S.O.S., and felt that the name Peter was connected to an orderly who had worked there of the same name. A patient, long dead, may still be asking for help from the orderly.

These are the types of experiences that inspire the Sisters of Salem to continue seeking answers to what may be unanswerable. How and why do the spirits of patients long dead choose to stay in their place of medical incarceration?

SOS will continue to visit St. Albans Sanatorium in search of those answers. After all, it is a location whose ghostly inhabitants are more than happy to engage with the living.

How patients viewed the outside world

Some of those who called St. Albans home would sit on this window seat and stare out into the mountains, or cool their eyes on the New River, which flowed directly in front of them. How many dreamed of fleeing the routine and dullness of sanatorium life by floating away on a boat down the winding, watery escape route that lay just out of

Is it time?

Time seems to stand

still inside St. Albans

Sanatorium.

Photo of graffiti on

the windowsill of a

bathroom located

across the hall from

Jacob's room.

CHAPTER 11
Dedicated to the Paranormal Field

ESP: El Con Society of the Paranormal

Team Founded: March 2009

Hometown: Bradenton, Florida

Founders: John Head (Doc), M.D., and Terri Rohde

Team Members: Marie Tufts, Earl Tufts, and Tracy Watts

Website: www.facebook.com/ESP.2009

El Con Society of the Paranormal (ESP) was founded by John K. Head, M.D., aka "Doc," and Terri Rohde. Although they have led the team into a number of haunted locations across America, St. Albans provided so much evidential experience that they found themselves visiting her dark halls over and over again.

"We have traveled from Florida to Radford, Virginia on four different occasions to investigate St. Albans," said Terri. During that time they have experienced a plethora of paranormal activity, including the sounds of disembodied voices, the vision of a full-body apparition, having an investigator slapped by an unseen hand, disembodied growling, and a disappearing door, among others.

Terri, Marie and Earl Tufts represented ESP during their first visit to the old asylum. It was during this stay at St. Albans that the group heard a young woman say, "Hi," as they were conducting an EVP session and then again, as they were leaving the building.

"We also heard footsteps overhead, when we were on the ground floor by the stairs," said Terri. "On our audio recorders during a 36 hour investigation, we captured the voice of a little girl saying, 'Where are we going?' We recorded this when we were taking a tour of the building with Dean Simpkins of Mountain Ridge Paranormal Research Society. He was telling us which door to exit from during the night and he was saying that if we heard the door alarm, it would be him running a security check," she said.

Finding a door to exit would become a puzzling exercise during one of their St. Albans investigations. Marie and Terri were in what is known as "the safe room," because a large old-fashioned safe is located there. They had completed their investigation and were readying to leave the room when they realized they couldn't. There wasn't a door. "It was as if it had been morphed over," said Marie. "We went around and around in circles. We were growing concerned when we made another lap and there it was. It was as if the door materialized out of nowhere," she added.

In addition to the physical manifestation of the power that is St. Albans Sanatorium's energy, Terri would find that the inhabitants of the old asylum liked her enough to cry out for her. She heard her name called by a spirit while she was on the grand staircase. This was not the last EVP the team would record.

Disappearing door

Two members of ESP experienced a very rare paranormal phenomena at St. Albans. After an investigation, when they were ready to leave, the door simply wasn't there. They walked several times around the room before the portal suddenly appeared.

On their most recent visit to St. Albans, the team was conducting an EVP session and asked if there were any spirits in the room and if so, what were their names. They picked up a female voice identifying itself as, "Debra." Not long after this incident, the team was talking about a new EMF "stuffed puppy dog" (electromagnetic field meter that is sensitive to touch). A spirit must have thought this was interesting, because they picked up a male voice giving an approval of the technology, "Nice."

Although a ghostly visit at St. Albans is something one does not forget, the team received a special welcome from an entity who found its home on that night disturbed by the curious supernatural sleuths. "My most memorable experience from this investigation was whenever a first time team member, who was a sensitive, and I went downstairs to the bowling alley area of the basement. The team had already discussed that if we heard a noise at any time, we would go toward the noise to try to debunk the sound," said Terri. She continued, "So, as we got to the bottom of the stairs we heard a faint growling noise. We all pointed in the same direction, so we began to go toward the noise. We heard it again and advanced toward the sound, when all of a sudden the growling began anew, but louder this time, much more aggressive and right in our faces."

This final auditory assault was too much for the young man who had been serving as their guide that night. He broke through the investigators who were standing between him and escape and began running up the stairs. At the same time he began to run, his MEL meter began screaming. (A MEL Meter measures both electromagnetic fields and temperature.) The rest of the investigators paused for just a second and then followed him up the stairs, each of them shouting as well. "When we arrived upstairs, the sensitive turned around and went to the top of the stairs and yelled back down the stairs, 'back off!' Suddenly, everything stopped. There was only an uneasy quietness that had settled over the room," said Terri.

The residents of St. Albans often seem to like to connect with certain individuals. Shortly after escaping from the aggressive energy in the basement, they heard a slapping sound and realized that the same young man who had broken through their ranks to run up the stairs after hearing the deep growling, had been whacked soundly in the head. "We all heard the slap and saw the man's head rock back from the blow," said Terri.

The Bowling Alley

It was here that members of the El Con Society of the Paranormal came face-to-face with an entity that let them know their presence was not welcomed. The growling they heard when they first encountered the being escalated to the point that the seasoned team members panicked and ran.

The encounter with the entity in the basement was only one of the highly unusual events that occurred while they were there. About 2:00 a.m., during the same visit on June 20, 2013, the team was downstairs in the boiler room engaged in an EVP session. This area is considered, by many who have investigated St. Albans, to be highly active. The team was trying to contact Gina Renee Hall or someone who knew what had happened to her.

Gina Hall was a young woman whose bloodstained car was found nearby on Hazel Hollow Road. She was murdered on June 28, 1980. The only witness was St. Albans Sanatorium and she is not one to give up her secrets. The perpetrator of Gina's death remains at-large.

It was during this session that the sensitive felt she had made contact with the spirit of Gina and that the girl was buried in concrete on the sanatorium's premises. She felt so strongly about this that she even requested that they call the police. "Because it was the first time we had investigated with her, we were hesitant to do so," said Terri. "Since investigating with her a number of times since, we've realized that she is very good with picking up on residual energy."

The police were never called. Only time and the deconstruction of St. Albans will reveal all her secrets. Whether Gina is one of those secrets, remains to be seen.

Interested supernatural detectives come from all over America to spend time within St. Albans' cold walls. Because of the broad spectrum of encounters with preternatural energy that occurs there, the El Con Society of the Paranormal has made the journey on several occasions. They will come again. They have to, St. Albans Sanatorium has called to them and they will answer.

CHAPTER 12
Its All in the Photographs

The Ghost Writers

Team Founded: August 2008

Hometown: Abingdon, Virginia

Founder: Pat Bussard O'Keefe

Team Members: Stephanie Bussard, Ken O'Keefe, Scarlett McGrady,
                   Megan Bussard, and Jon Matney

Auxilary Members: Pam Wilson Berry, Leigh Shilling Edwards, and
                   Cheyenne McGrady

Website: www.theghost-writers.com

To those who are open to it and who seek out the company of ghosts, it is always thrilling to record evidence of a haunting on film. This euphoric feeling is multiplied when the site in which this evidence is captured is as lovely and haunted as St. Albans Sanatorium.

It was during a photo session on November 1, 2014, for which the author and founder of the Ghost Writers, Pat Bussard O'Keefe was shooting for After Dark Magazine, that she recorded a most unusual anomaly. Pat photographed a mist forming from a nondescript shape into a very distinct humanoid-looking head. Sections from two of these photos are featured later in this chapter. Keep in mind that as a photographer, Pat O'Keefe is the first to say that any visual images captured by a device with multiple pieces of glass making up the whole, can be due to light happily bouncing in a crazy manner throughout the lens. What she can also say is that after taking literally tens of thousands of photos at reportedly haunted locations across America, she has never shot another anomaly quite like this curious formation of what might be a ghost or entity forming right in front of the camera.

The location of this spectacular piece of possible paranormal activity took place on the third floor of the massive structure. The site of this photo was taken near the lavatory known as the suicide bathroom. The location was not far from where EVPs are often captured of a woman, who having lost her baby through premature delivery, was allowed to keep it in a jar in the closet. The doctor felt that it would be excellent therapy for the grieving mother.

The third floor, or attic area as it is also called, is a place known for some pretty dark energy. In fact, the location is darker and has a more oppressive feel to it than many of the other locations of purported haunted activity around the building and grounds. In spite of that, it is an energy that draws those who are curious about what lies beyond the universe of the living.

The day the anomaly was photographed, St. Albans Sanatorium was wrapping up its annual Halloween haunted house. Each year, the volunteers and staff of the old asylum choose a theme for the event. In 2014, it was *The House of Havoc.*

Sanatorium of shadows and light

Looking down the hallway, first door on the left, was the lonely sanctuary of a mother doomed to hold her baby closely to her, in a most horrific manner.
The hallway was shot in close proximity to what is known as the suicide bathroom.

The lead character was one, Dr. Havoc, played by the talented Jenny Johnston. It was in the photos of Jenny/Dr. Havoc that the anomaly presented. The image was so striking, that Pat O'Keefe spotted the phantom image in the photos well before completing the entire shoot. At the time, she was with Ken O'Keefe, Jeffrey Miller, Eden Biggs, Jenny Johnston, and several more volunteer members, preparing to shoot a scene with Connor Mullins. Mullins was modeling that night as one of Dr. Havoc's victims for the shoot. As Pat was going through some of the photos she had already shot, the misty images of the being as it developed into a more solid body of substance were immediately noticeable in the pictures. She shared what she saw in the viewfinder with several of those present including Jeffrey, Jenny, and Ken.

If the reader would like to see the photos in their entirety, they can go view them as a video on YouTube at: https://www.youtube.com/watch?v=mfOGVFB5QQs. The Ghost Writers YouTube channels are "gh0stwriters" (use a zero for the 0) and "HauntedPhotographer."

Because of the size and shape of the images, Pat couldn't help but wonder, "Is this a ghost or an entity?" Ghosts and entities are two different things. Basically, one has lived and died as a human, the other was never connected as a living human spirit to the corporeal world. Some investigators, researchers, and lay people would call some of these entities negative energies, dark energies, or even demons.

Ghost, negative energy or, an aberration within the lens of a camera, are all possibilities. "I present the photographs within this chapter and will let the reader decide for him or herself," said Pat.

This was not the last time that members of their band of paranormal investigators had the good fortune to record a possible paranormal event. Their team, the Ghost Writers, has differentiated itself in the field through their preservation of historical places of supernatural repute through both images and the written word. Pat is the founder of this unit of preternatural explorers and this book is an example of what is at the core of the team's mission, safeguarding paranormal history.

They have travelled far and wide to a number of places of preternatural repute. St. Albans is one that haunts their minds and hearts.

Many locations identify themselves as having a haunted reputation. St. Albans is one of the few sites of the number that these investigators have visited that lived up to its hype.

Ectoplasm?

The photos to the left and right were part of a series taken in sequence that appeared to show a white mist developing into a humanoid form.

As an example, on Sunday, September 27, 2015, Pat was at the sanatorium with team members Ken O'Keefe, Scarlett McGrady, and Megan Bussard. The purpose of their visit that day was to photograph SAS one last time, to complete the photo list needed before the book was to go to print.

Because the sanatorium was once again dressed in her garb as a haunted house, there were few places within the building that could be photographed without the backdrop of Halloween props. However, one area remained unadorned by the trappings of the season, the birdcage.

At approximately 3:30 p.m., Pat, Scarlett, and Megan left the area outside of Director of Operations, Marcelle Hanauer's office to go to the cage to photograph the location for The Ghosts of St. Albans Sanatorium and to conduct a short EVP session. They traveled through the door to the purple room, turned left and went up the steps. The trio had to slip under a tarp in order to gain access to the area. The staircase had been covered with a tarpaulin to keep Halloween haunted house thrill seekers from ascending to the second floor via that route.

When the investigators came to the landing, The first thing they were struck with was how cold it had gotten. Scarlett was the first one to mention this fact and the other two investigators immediately agreed.

Pat, who had been to St. Albans on a dozen different occasions and who was somewhat familiar with the building, immediately took a left hand turn. She began looking for the hallway that would take them to their destination. "It was absolutely the strangest thing, I looked for the hallway and it just flat out wasn't there," said Pat. The other two investigators with her watched her go down the length of the short corridor looking for the connecting hallway , but were unable to see it either.

"I was totally confused, I knew it was supposed to be there, but it wasn't," said Pat. "I had even asked Shelli Sprouse Meade, a St. Albans historian and volunteer who was there that day, where the location of the birdcage was before leaving the conference area of the building. I wanted to make sure we were going to the correct part of the building," she said.

Unnerved, Pat, Scarlett, and Megan turned and followed the hallway to the classroom. This is a location in the building that was recreated to resemble a schoolroom, which was part of St. Albans first incarnation. It is thought by many in the paranormal field that spirits will sometimes respond to something that was familiar to them when they were in the world of the living.

Disappearing hallway

The entrance to this wide and well-lit hallway had disappeared during a time when three paranormal investigators went in search of the Birdcage.

They were in the classroom for about 20 minutes. During this time, Pat took several photographs, while Scarlett and Megan conducted a short EVP session.

When they came out of the room and started down the hallway, the whole corridor was visible, to the other end. And, right where it should have been, so was the hallway to the cage.

Pat immediately went to the location and took several photographs of the massive and brightly lit hallway. The very one that wasn't visible less than a half hour before.

Scarlett once again brought the temperature of the room to the attention of the other two investigators. "Do you feel how much warmer it is in here now?" asked Scarlett. According to www.weatherunderground.com/history, the temperature was in the low 60s that day.

On Saturday, October 3, 2015, Pat contacted Shelli Sprouse Meade, who wrote part of the first chapter, *Repository of Souls: The History of St. Albans Sanatorium*, to check on the timeline of the birdcage hallway. "The hallway as it is now, wasn't constructed until 1916," said Shelli. According to the St. Albans website, www.stalbans-virginia.com, "It was in 1916 that Dr. J.C. King converted St. Albans from a boy's school to an asylum for the mentally ill and St. Albans Sanatorium came into existence."

Pat sent the photograph, which can be seen on the preceding page, to Shelli. She identified the location on the photograph of the original, very short, and very dark hallway as ending at the point before the open door of the lavatory. This room and the others along the way to the cage can be shown spilling light, and lots of it, into the corridor.

Why were the three women unable to see such a large and bright hallway? Could it have been a slip in time, where for just a moment, they walked from one era into another? Did they step from one parallel dimension to another? Or, is there another explanation for what they experienced? Whatever the answer, it is an experience that none of the three of them will ever forget.

This is only the latest experience the author has had with St. Albans' powerful energy. The first time Pat saw the sanatorium, she felt there was something special about the building and grounds. "You can literally feel the energy as it comes off the outside walls in waves. She is at once beautiful and deadly, light and dark, those who walk her hallways would do well to avoid

Powerful energy
Almost completely
hidden by a canopy
of trees, the New
River is shown
flowing beneath the
steady gaze of the
sanatorium.

being lulled into a sense of safety, or what happened to a member of Mountain Ridge Paranormal Research Society (MRPRS) could happen to them," said Pat.

Several years ago, she was writing and photographing St. Albans for <u>Ghost Voices Magazine</u> and she interviewed a member of the paranormal investigation team, MRPRS, whose story is told in the second chapter of this book. He told Pat a story about standing beneath a tree located outside and to the far right of St. Albans. From this vantage one can see the beautiful New River. This ancient water source provides a steady source of power for the Denizens hiding behind the doors and windows of the old sanatorium. The power that phantoms can pull from this hydro-energy source also allows them to roam its grounds, as this unfortunate individual found out. Standing beneath the tree, Chuck Thornton heard his name called and when he turned around in response, he was slapped soundly across his face. Not a pleasant greeting from this grand old lady.

Not everyone is ready to investigate St. Albans Sanatorium in their search for the shades of those who have passed from life to death. Even seasoned investigators should prepare and keep their guard up and wits about them as they tread these hallways with the bravado of those of their kind. For, should she decide to make a point that she is not one to be taken lightly, the memory of an encounter with her can be . . . a nightmare.

Spirit Encounter

The tree and location where Chuck Thornton of the Mountain Ridge Paranormal Research Society said he heard his name called. When he turned to see who was calling him, an unknown spirit or entity slapped him, hard.

Near the skylight walkway

This area and to the right was where patients could be found playing cards,

or enjoying the caress of the sun as it flowed through skylights, painting the

sanatorium in shades of yellow and gold.

CHAPTER 13
Saving St Albans

St. Albans
Sanatorium

Shhhh. No one can hear you scream.

The staff of St. Albans Sanatorium is ingenious when it comes to fundraising for their cause. "We hold any number of events to raise money for St. Albans," said Marcelle Hanauer, director of operations for the sanatorium.

Over the years that has meant a dedicated cadre of volunteers was needed to man activities as diverse as zombie walks, history tours, and the wildly successful haunted house. "These events raise funds for renovations to St. Albans," said Marcelle. "I am so proud of all of the work that our volunteers do to help save the sanatorium. Without them, the restoration that we have done thus far would not have been possible."

The work that these many volunteers have done has resulted in new windows and much-needed repairs to the roof, in addition to paint and a thousand other structural details. Led by Bruce Barraclough, Jr., a number of volunteers recently rebuilt the stairs to the grand staircase.

"There have been so many volunteers over the years and we just want them to know how appreciated they are for all the work they've done," said Marcelle. Although much has been done to save St. Albans, there is still much to do and the events offered to a paying public are plentiful and varied.

One of the most important of these events is the annual Halloween haunted house. Each year, the sanatorium offers up a fresh cauldron of horrific characters and fun scenarios to populate the rooms of the former asylum. The theme for the 2015 year was *Unchained* and brought out a record number of thrill seekers. They were not disappointed as a volunteer cadre of the dead and undead strove to make their visit to the energetic old asylum memorable.

Haunted Houses

These events are a vital component of the fundraising strategy to raise money for renovations to St. Albans Sanatorium.

The sanatorium's haunted houses are an All Soul's Eve season's legend in the region and beyond. Many visitors to these events come more than once.

Other sanatorium events brewed from the imaginations of SAS staff and volunteers are the highly successful *Zombie Apocalypse Simulation Games*. With the advent of the undead staggering once again into popular culture, the thought of an exercise where someone can escape the ravenous mouths of these relentless killers appeals to some.

"We have people who come back time-and-time again," said Marcelle. "Using their wits and speed to outmaneuver an opponent like this in a zombie apocalypse simulation game gives players a sense of what their favorite television characters would experience in the real world."

The former sanatorium is the perfect place to run a gauntlet filled with these fantastical decaying monsters. There are dark corners and half-closed doors everywhere throughout the closed asylum, perfect hiding places for these shuffling jaws of death.

Zombies are just part of the fun at St. Albans, *Flashlight Ghost Walk*s are also a component of the gleeful connection to the ghosts and entities that dwell at the sanatorium. These tours are usually of shorter duration, two hours in length, and provide a dark introduction to the building, without the investment of a lengthier residence at the sanatorium.

If just a couple of hours is not enough to quench one's thirst for an encounter with the Denizens of the bygone asylum, there are *Public Paranormal Investigations*. These exciting excursions into the depths of the sanatorium in search of paranormal activity are perfect for the preternatural enthusiast.

The public investigations usually last from 8:00 p.m. until past the Witching Hour, ending at 1:00 a.m. The cost is minimal and gives the interested supernatural sleuth time to really get in touch with some of St. Albans' inhabitants.

For the serious paranormal investigator, the sanatorium offers overnight and 36 hour investigations. These investigations are open to a minimum of 10 people. Teams may be smaller, but will incur the total charge for the investigation. In addition, teams can be no larger than 20. Team members must complete a registration/liability form prior to entering the building. A tour of the building is provided prior to the investigation.

Investigators must be 18 years or older to participate. At this time, participants do not have to purchase individual liability insurance.

Horror characters inhabit the sanatorium

During its annual Halloween Haunted House, St. Albans

plays host to a number of terrifying new characters.

Photograph by Magen King, Queen of a King Photography

In addition to these macabre activities, there are a plethora of other events to scare, titillate, and educate the interested spirit seeker.

For those who are uninterested in things that go bump in the night, or who choose to avoid the energetic buzz of an adrenaline rush, the sanatorium offers *History Tours*. Participants taking part in these tours step back in time to learn about St. Albans during each of her incarnations.

These educational history tours provide a snapshot of the day-to-day operation of the sanatorium. "St. Albans has such a long and distinguished history," said Marcelle. "We hear comments from clients all the time about how interesting the tours are because of what they learned about the sanatorium and about the early beginnings of psychiatry," she said.

These are just a handful of events that St. Albans staff and volunteers develop and coordinate on a regular basis. These hard working people are dedicated to restoring an important piece of history. Check the calendar online to see what events and activities are available at www.stalbans-virginia.com.

In a very real sense, the staff, volunteers and all those who back the asylum through their support of these events and more, are trying to save St. Albans, one ticket at a time.

Beware of Zombies!

As part of its fundraising repertoire, St. Albans sponsors thrilling events throughout the year like Zombie Apocalypse Simulation Games.

In appreciation
of –

Jessica O'Dell,

St. Albans

Sanatorium

former volunteer

coordinator and

co-founder of the

Mountain Ridge

Paranormal Research

Society,

on the grand

staircase.

Appendix

Floor Plans

     St. Albans Sanatorium is made up of a labyrinth of hallways and rooms. Architectural drawings were added to the book so that readers can connect with the locations of haunted activity that were reported taking place throughout the building and property.

St Albans Sanatorium

First Floor

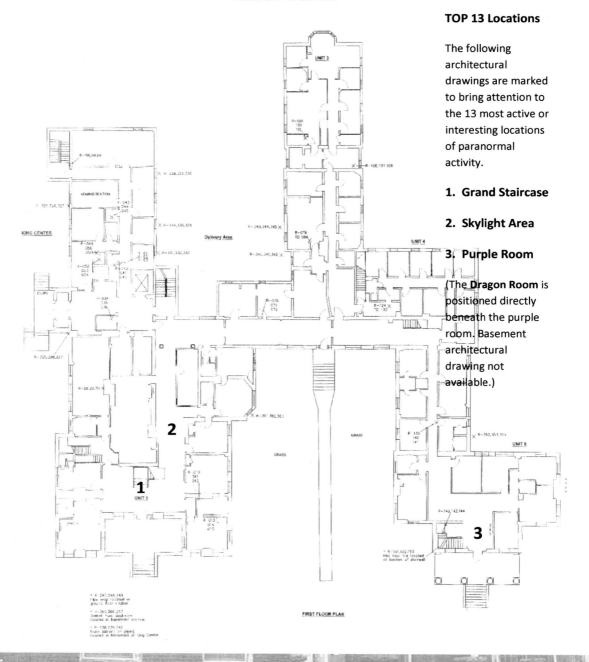

TOP 13 Locations

The following architectural drawings are marked to bring attention to the 13 most active or interesting locations of paranormal activity.

1. **Grand Staircase**

2. **Skylight Area**

3. **Purple Room**

(The **Dragon Room** is positioned directly beneath the purple room. Basement architectural drawing not available.)

FIRST FLOOR PLAN

St Albans Sanatorium

Second Floor

4. **Donald's Room**

5. **Jacob's Room**

6. **Disappearing Hallway**

7. **The Cage/Birdcage**

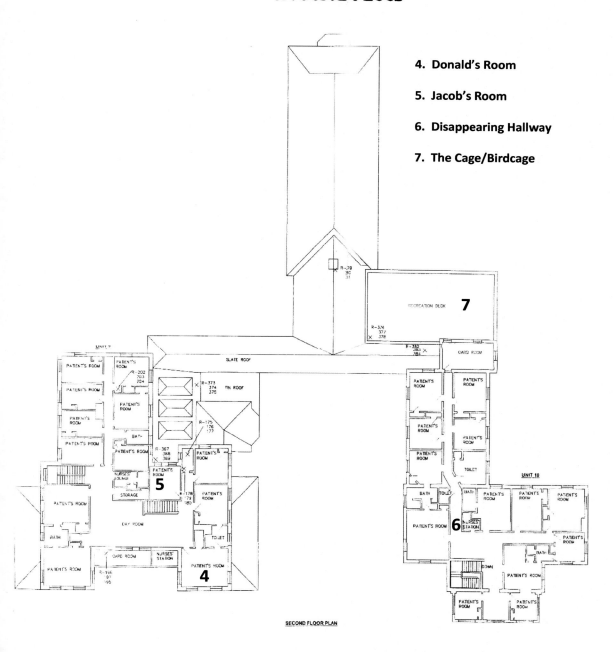

SECOND FLOOR PLAN

St. Albans Sanatorium

Third Floor

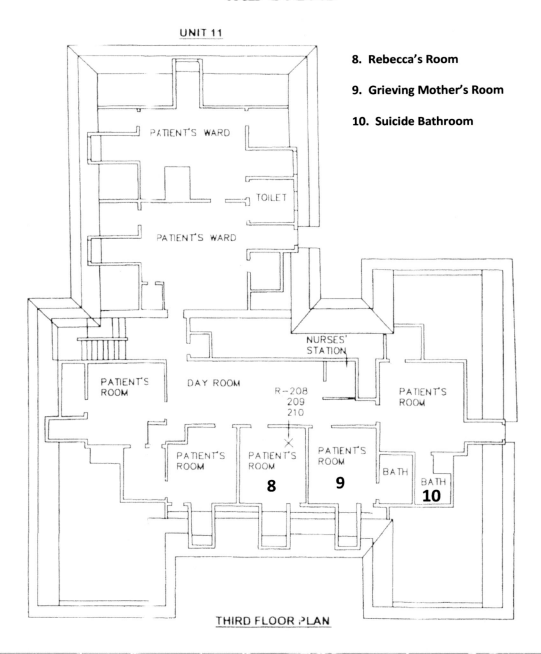

8. Rebecca's Room
9. Grieving Mother's Room
10. Suicide Bathroom

St Albans Sanatorium

King Center

Basement

11. **File Room**

12. **Boiler Room**

13. **Bowling Alley**

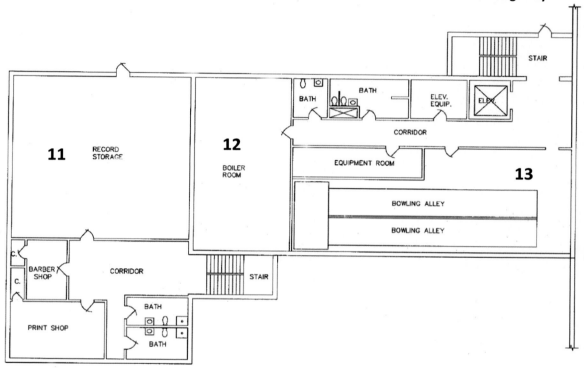

BASEMENT FLOOR
KING CENTER
St.Albans Campus

NOVEMBER 2001

SCALE: 1/16"=1'-0"

St Albans Sanatorium
King Center
First/Main Floor

Alcoholics' Wing

Hydrotheraphy

Electroshock 14

Electroshock Recovery

Long Hallway

14. Electroshock Therapy

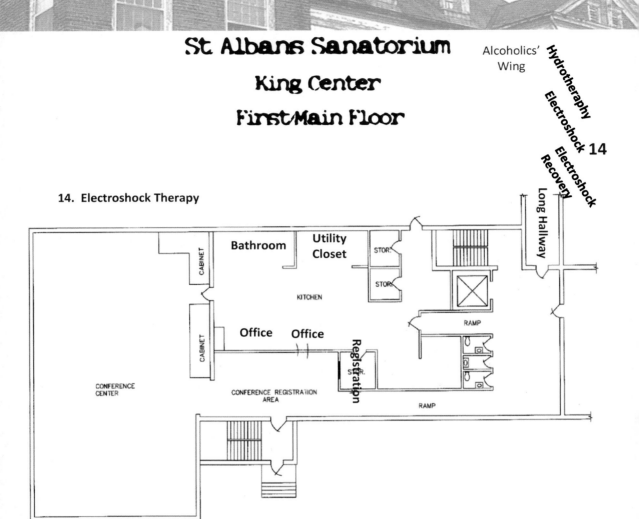

Bathroom

Utility Closet

STOR.

STOR.

KITCHEN

CABINET

CABINET

Office

Office

RAMP

CONFERENCE CENTER

CONFERENCE REGISTRATION AREA

Registration

STOR.

RAMP

MAIN FLOOR
KING CENTER
St.Albans Campus

MAY 03

St Albans Sanatorium
King Center
Second Floor

15. 2nd Floor KC Hallway

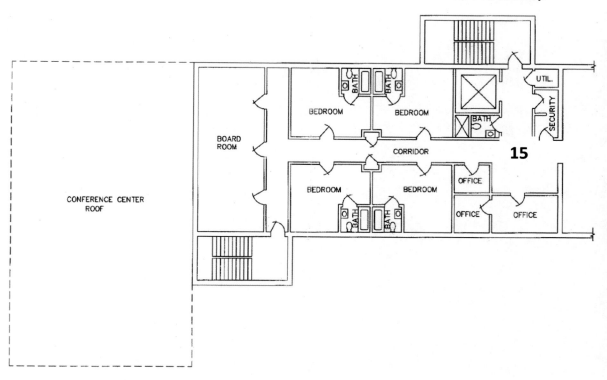

CONFERENCE CENTER ROOF

BOARD ROOM

BEDROOM

BEDROOM

BATH

BATH

CORRIDOR

15

UTIL.

SECURITY

BATH

BEDROOM

BEDROOM

BATH

BATH

OFFICE

OFFICE

OFFICE

NOVEMBER 2001

SECOND FLOOR
KING CENTER
St.Albans Campus

SCALE: 1/16"=1'-0"

Ruined Asylum

She stands
sentinel to echoes
of souls distressed
withering and trapped
within prison walls
eternal night prevails

She hides
misery, loss, death
of spirits silenced
in dark hallways
rooms sunlit starved
voices quieted eternally

She screams
in muted voice to all comers
within her bowels
time jumps erratically
space expands, contracts

She welcomes
all foolish visitors
and unwise are all
who enter through
doors, broken windows
to find her waiting

For her spirit is eternal
and faithful
and she will hold you to her
Forever.

Ruined Asylum from **Boneyard Voice,** 2016, a collection of poetry by Pat Bussard O'Keefe.

A final glance . . .

This book was developed to preserve a piece of legendary paranormal history through stories and photographs. St. Albans Sanatorium is a location that sears herself into the memory of all those who have had the good fortune to visit her. Like other notable locations situated across all dimensions of time and space, she is impossible to forget.

Photograph by Magen King, Queen of a King Photography

Unwillingly Channeled

"I was leading a group through the sanatorium with another volunteer when something took over me. I blacked out and fell on the stairs. The next thing I know, they are carrying me outside. Once everyone got outside, the front door slammed shut behind us. I'll never forget that."

Matt Collins

Shawsville, VA.

St. Albans Sanatorium rooftop

Scene from the Long Hallway.

View of the courtyard area.

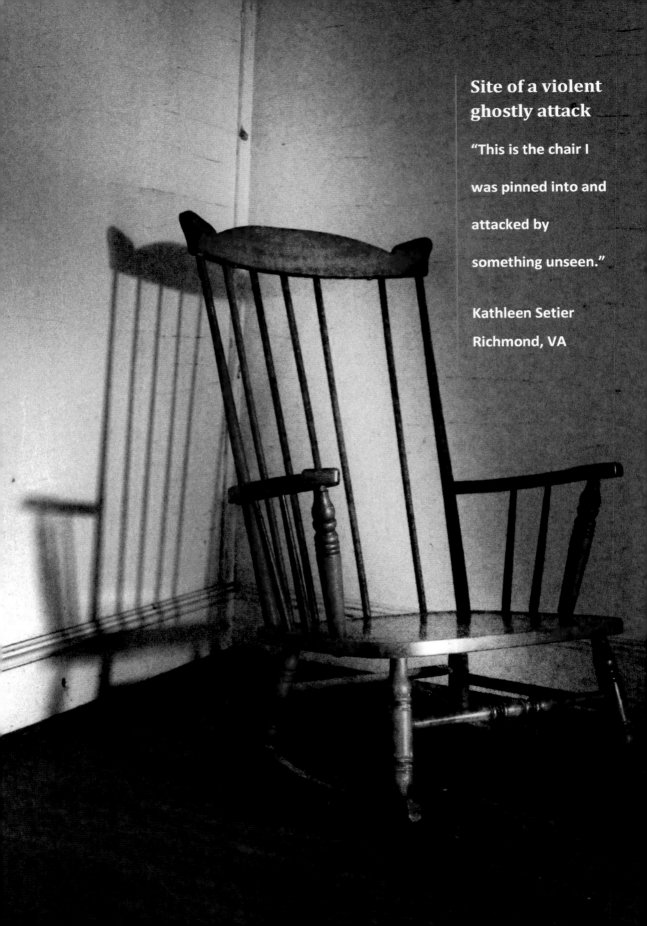

Site of a violent ghostly attack

"This is the chair I

was pinned into and

attacked by

something unseen."

Kathleen Setier
Richmond, VA

The view from the front porch, riverside.

A glimpse of the cage from the yard.

House of Havoc

A scene featuring a murdering clown, a character from the 2014 haunted house experience.

The being was feeding off my reaction

"My wife, Tonya, and I were on the second floor hallway (known as 'crawler alley') when a being dropped, upside down, directly in front of me. The thing then flashed a terrible grin, like it was feeding off of my reaction. I will never forget that terrifying encounter."

Eric Perry
Founder, Haunted in New England
Manchester, New Hampshire

The skylight area

Second floor

Area in front of the
grand staircase

On June 28, 1980 the heinous murder of Gina Renee Hall was committed not far from St Albans and her bloodstained car was found only a few hundred yards away on Hazel Hollow Road.

From chapter 1, "Repository of Souls: History of St. Albans Sanatorium."

Courtesy of St. Albans Sanatorium.

Hallway, first floor

A scene from the corridor connecting the two sides of the building.

Shadow people are often reported walking the hallways of the asylum.

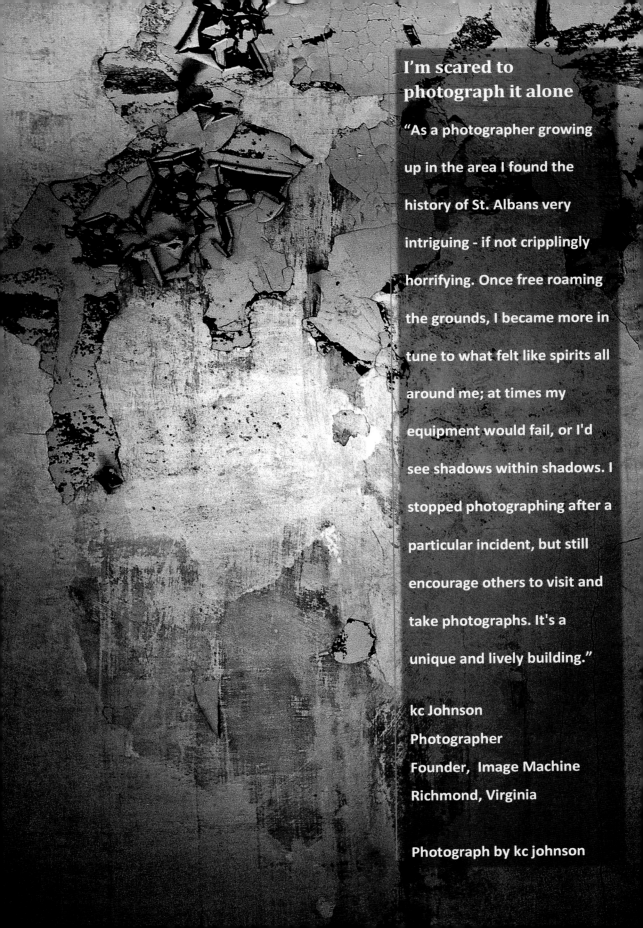

I'm scared to photograph it alone

"As a photographer growing up in the area I found the history of St. Albans very intriguing - if not cripplingly horrifying. Once free roaming the grounds, I became more in tune to what felt like spirits all around me; at times my equipment would fail, or I'd see shadows within shadows. I stopped photographing after a particular incident, but still encourage others to visit and take photographs. It's a unique and lively building."

kc Johnson
Photographer
Founder, Image Machine
Richmond, Virginia

Photograph by kc johnson

Courtyard view

Conference Center windows

In Jacob's room

We heard a girl scream

"During a zombie apocalypse event, Angela Collins and I were in the pink room when we heard a girl's scream come across a walkie talkie. No one else heard the cry for help.

"This made everyone uncomfortable, so Chuck Thornton moved us upstairs. At that point a crutch, which had been resting against a wall, was thrown across the room. This startled everyone, so, we relocated to the connecting hallway. At that point, A tarp hanging over a doorway began moving like it was breathing."

Jeffrey Miller
(Pictured in character for a St. Albans haunted house.)
Pulaski, Virginia

www.stalbans-virginia.com

www.patbussard.com